MEXICAN COOKING

MEXICAN COOKING

ROGER HICKS

APPLE

A QUINTET BOOK

Published by The Apple Press
6 Blundell Street
London N7 9BH

Copyright © 1990 Quintet Publishing Limited.
All rights reserved. No part of this publication may be
reproduced, stored in a retrieval system or transmitted
in any form or by any means, electronic, mechanical,
photocopying, recording or otherwise, without the
permission of the copyright holder.

ISBN 1-85076-474-3

Reprinted 1993, 1995, 1996

This book was designed and produced by
Quintet Publishing Limited
6 Blundell Street
London N7 9BH

Creative Director: Peter Bridgewater
Art Director: Ian Hunt
Designer: Annie Moss
Artwork: Danny McBride
Editor: Barbara Fuller

Typeset in Great Britain by
Central Southern Typesetters, Eastbourne
Manufactured in Hong Kong by
Regent Publishing Services Limited
Printed in Singapore by
Star Standard Industries Pte. Ltd.

CONTENTS

COCINA MEXICANA

The best Mexican food is rarely found in restaurants, even in Mexico. It is a unique blend of Central American, of Spanish, and of the Arab cooking which in its turn influenced Spain. It can be brutally simple, or extremely complex: indeed, the same dish may well be prepared in ways which reflect the various influences in very varying degrees, so you may have an Aztec version, a poor Spanish soldiers' version, a rich hidalgo's version, and a Moorish version.

For the most part, though, Mexican cookery uses a relatively limited number of techniques, and a relatively limited number of ingredients, and it is not difficult to learn. It may be time-consuming, but anyone who likes to cook will have an excellent chance of complete success the first time they try to cook a dish. Also, Mexican food is mostly cheap, delicious and filling: it is as suitable for a student dinner-party as for a gathering of older and more well-to-do gastronomes.

Admittedly, there are some things which are easily available in Mexico itself, or in the south-western United States, that are much harder to come by in other parts of the world. Corn tortillas are one of the best examples. In Mexico, at the time of writing, they were about 1000 pesos a kilo: say 25¢ a pound in US currency. In California, in the shops the Mexicans patronize, fresh corn tortillas might run to twice that. In Britain, small cans of tortillas cost approximately ten times the price of the Mexican version.

You can, however, compromise and improvise. In Mexico, tortillas de harina (flour tortillas) are much more expensive than corn tortillas – but flour tortillas are just as authentic, and are actually cheaper to make in many places. Or, if you live near an Indian shop, you can buy chapattis: these are so similar to some types of Mexican tortillas that you would never know the difference. In fact, if you live near an Indian shop, you will find that many of the spices and ingredients (especially the various kinds of chilli peppers) are suitable for use in Mexican cookery. There's more about finding ingredients, and making substitutions, elsewhere in the book.

One very important point is that Mexican food is not all mouth-blisteringly hot. By choosing the types and quantities of chillies that you use, you can vary the style of the food from mild to *muy picante*. It is however worth remembering that you can rapidly build up a tolerance for food that is *muy picante*, and that if you invite unsuspecting friends over to try a favourite recipe that you have made a number of times, you may make it in a way that makes their eyes water!

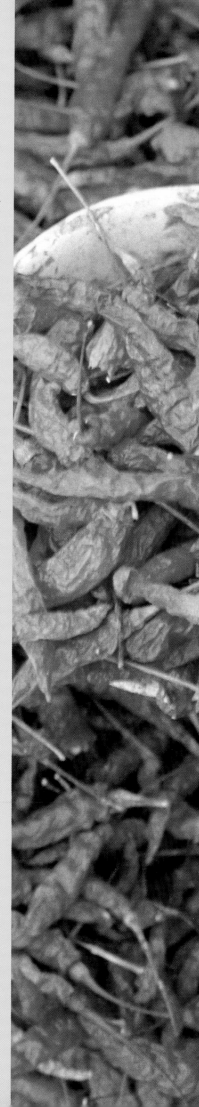

NO HAY REGLAS FIJAS

'*No hay reglas fijas*' – there are no fixed rules. This applies to many aspects of Mexican life, as anyone who has tried to drive through central Tijuana will attest, but it is arguably most true in Mexican cooking.

There are two main reasons for this. One is the inventiveness of the Mexican people, born partly of necessity and partly of sheer natural exuberance: you work with what you've got, and you modify any recipe to make it closer to what you want. The other is the sheer size and diversity of Mexico. The border with the United States is over 1,800 miles long, and the country is more than a thousand miles from north to south. Add to this the fact that there are tropical and sub-tropical coastal areas (the 'Tierra Calda'), the temperate plateaux (the 'Tierra Templada') and the cold high mountains (the 'Tierra Fria'); allow for the mountain ranges which for centuries separated one valley from the next; and you will see that the scope for regional and local variations in recipes is enormous.

If, therefore, the recipes in this book differ greatly from the recipes in another book, it is by no means unlikely that *both* are authentic. If you want to modify any recipe, for example by making it hotter or cooler or doubling the meat or halving the coriander, the chances are that it will still be authentic in the sense that someone, somewhere in Mexico, cooks it like that. As long as you stick to believable Mexican ingredients, whatever you cook will taste Mexican.

In fact, Mexican cooking (like most other types of cooking) is more a state of mind than a matter of following recipes slavishly. In so far as there are any rules, there are two things worth remembering. The first is that Mexicans often cook meat for far longer than North Americans or northern Europeans do: often, meat is boiled for hours, until it can be shredded with two forks, before it is added to the vegetables or *mole* (sauce). The second thing to remember is that you can ring the changes by using different meats (beef, pork, chicken, lamb or even goat) in one sauce, or by using different sauces with the same meat.

7

INGREDIENTS

There are several ingredients which give Mexican cookery its characteristic flavours and which it is almost impossible to do without. If there isn't a Mexican shop handy, some of these things should be available at any good supermarket, while others may require a bit of hunting. As already mentioned, Indian shops are a good place to look; so are Chinese and other oriental shops. See also the Glossary on pages 94/95.

AVOCADOS There are far more varieties of avocado in Mexico than in most parts of the world, and they usually come to the market in better condition: ripe, and superbly flavoured. The ones with the thick, knobbly skins (Hass) are generally the best varieties outside Mexico. A ripe avocado yields to gentle finger pressure without being squashy or blackened. Underripe avocados, provided they were not picked too early, will improve if they are left in a bowl in the kitchen, preferably with a couple of bananas for company.

CHAYOTE Pear-shaped gourd or squash.

CHEESES AND MILK PRODUCTS

There are dozens, perhaps hundreds, of kinds of Mexican cheese. Some are made from cows' milk, some from goats'

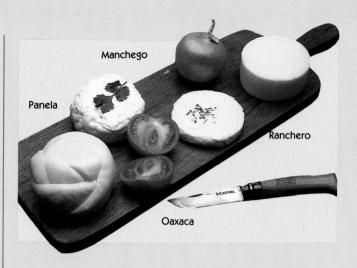

ABOVE: Mexican cheeses. BELOW: Dried Chillies.

milk. If you can't get authentic Mexican cheeses, you can use Jack (or failing that, Cheddar) for most purposes where the cheese has to be melted, and sour cream as a substitute for the Mexican cream or 'crema agria' that is so often used as a garnish in Mexico.

CHILLIES According to whom you believe, there are between 50 and 250 varieties of chilli peppers used in Mexican cooking. For our purposes, there are four groups. Inside each group, substitutions are normally possible. ***Fresh hot chillies*** SERRANO and JALAPENO chillies are the best-known here; they are very hot indeed. Generally,

they are interchangeable. Use two or three of the smaller serranos in place of a single larger jalapeno. When cutting these, wash your hands and the knife blade carefully afterwards: rubbing your eyes with a chilli-contaminated finger is an agonizing experience, though you are unlikely to do yourself any lasting harm.

Fresh large chillies These are much milder: the big ANAHEIM and POBLANO chillies are only slightly hotter than bell peppers (green peppers). The seeds and veins (in which the heat chiefly resides) are removed before use: see Chilli Preparation (page 15).

Dried chillies All of these are hot, though the small red ones are much hotter than the big brownish, dark red or black CALIFORNIAS, NEW MEXICOS, ANCHOS, PASILLAS, NEGROS etc. Many are available powdered. Seeds and veins are usually removed from the larger chillies (see page 15), but not the smaller ones.

Other prepared chillies Various forms of pickled chillies are available. Many recipes call for pickled jalapenos, though fresh peppers can be substituted, while pickled chillies in sauce (EN ESCABECHE) add a unique flavour of their own. CHIPOTLE chillies are smoked, and usually sold en escabeche.

CHOCOLATE Central America is the home of chocolate. Mainly used as a drink, it is also used in making chocolate mole sauce for savoury dishes (page 81).

ABOVE: A basketful of chillies and peppers BELOW: Fresh chillies.

CORIANDER Fresh coriander or 'Chinese parsley' ('cilantro' in Spanish) is used in many salsas and in several other kinds of cooking, and as a garnish. Ask for *dhaniya* in Hindi, or grow your own: coriander seeds will sprout, and fresh-picked coriander (with green coriander seeds) adds an extra dimension to salsa cruda.

Bell

Anaheim/ California

Poblano

Serrano

Wax

Jalapeno

Jicama · Chayote · Corn, dried and fresh · Nopales (pricklypear cactus) · Tomatoes · Burro bananas · Plantanos machos

Cilantro (coriander) · Avocado · Calabacitas (zucchini) · Limes · Red (mild) onion · Brown onion · Almonds · Pipian (pumpkin seeds) · Tamarind pod

CORN-HUSKS Not strictly an ingredient, these are used to wrap tamales (page 78) while cooking; they are discarded before eating. They are normally available only in Mexican stores.

HERBS AND SPICES Apart from chillies, the main herbs and spices used in Mexican food are oregano and black pepper. Fresh oregano (and sage and thyme, for that matter) are much more aromatic than the dried herbs. Don't use old spices that have been sitting on your shelf for years: throw them out and buy more, if they have lost their aromatic scent.

HOMINY This is maize treated with lye; it tastes surprisingly different from untreated maize. It comes in various forms, including the old Southern 'hominy grits', and canned. One of its main uses is in pozole (page 70).

JICAMA A root vegetable, with an unusual flavour something between a raw potato or turnip, an apple, and a sweet radish.

MASA This is the ready-mixed corn dough from which tortillas and tamales are made. If you can't get masa, you may be able to get the flour or dry mix called masa harina, which is *not* the same as cornflour and then make your own. Otherwise, you are going to have to buy your tortillas and tamales ready made.

PILONCILLO Coarse, partially refined sugar. Also available in Indian stores as *gur* or *jaggery*.

PIPIAN Raw, unsalted pumpkin seeds. These are used (like other nuts) for thickening and flavouring sauces and stews. You may find these in some Mexican shops: otherwise, you will need to slaughter and dress your own pumpkin.

PLANTANOS Banana-like fruit used instead of bananas in cooking. It never becomes quite as sweet as a banana, but it breaks up less in stews. Use very slightly unripe bananas if you can't find these. Called 'plantains' in West Indian stores.

READY-MADE FOODS There are recipes for both corn and flour tortillas on pages 16–17, but most people find it easier to buy ready-made as most Mexicans do. Unless you have a mould or former, it is also easier to buy taco shells, but there is no point in buying tostadas when it is so easy to fry tortillas and make them at home.

Many kinds of salsa can be bought ready-made, but these are much better if you make them yourself: it is not difficult, and there are several recipes on pages 22–7. Serve with freshly fried tostaditas (page 16) to see how chips and salsa *should* taste. Store-bought guacamole (page 23) is rarely a patch on home-made.

Refried beans are readily available canned, and are perfectly adequate. The first time you try freshly made frijoles refritos, though, you realize how much better they can be.

Innumerable other prepared Mexican foods are available from a wide variety of manufacturers, and many of them are astonishingly good: chocolate mole sauce, for example, is at least as good as you'll get in most restaurants. Home-made is even better, though!

Canned and frozen burritos, tamales, enchiladas etc. are mostly edible, but they don't bear much resemblance to the real things, especially when these are made properly.

TAMARIND Seed pod of the tamarind plant. Used to make an astringent drink, and in some dressings. Available in some Mexican, Indian and oriental shops.

TOMATILLOS These look rather like green tomatoes with a brown, papery husk. They are essential for some dishes, and green tomatoes are *not* a substitute.

IN THE KITCHEN

You do not need a fancy *batterie de cuisine* for Mexican cookery: indeed, the traditional earthenware *cazuelas* (casseroles) and *ollas* (pots) are a lot less convenient than modern utensils.

The most useful single cooking-pot is a large, heavy 'Dutch oven' or flameproof casserole: this replaces the clay olla which for centuries was the main cooking-pot of all Central American cultures. You also need a heavy skillet or large frying-pan (cast iron is ideal). Another smaller skillet and a saucepan or two will equip you to cook almost anything you like.

A selection of bowls of varying sizes, a couple of sharp knives, and a cutting board are necessary for food preparation.

Traditionally, a pestle and mortar were used to pound and purée food, and a large, strong pestle and mortar will make life very much easier today; add a second, smaller one for spices if you like.

Among electrical appliances, a blender is virtually essential: this makes it far easier to purée sauces to the degree of liquidity that is required. A food processor may be useful, but it cannot produce a fine enough purée for many applications. For grinding spices, a small electric coffee-mill is ideal – but don't use it for coffee afterward without thorough cleaning, or you will get some very strange flavours with your breakfast.

There are a few basic techniques which are applicable in many recipes, and which are easiest to cover here.

Chilli Preparation The larger dried chillies (ancho, California, New Mexico, etc) are first de-seeded and de-veined: the veins along the inside of the flesh contain much of the heat. Then, tear them into reasonably flat pieces, and toast them briefly on a hot, dry frying-pan or griddle. Hold them down for a few seconds, until they change colour and crackle. Then flip them over and hold the other side down for a few seconds. Do not allow them to burn, or they will become bitter.

12

Next, put the shredded, toasted chillies in a bowl, and just cover them with boiling water. Put a saucer on top to hold them under water, and leave to soak for at least half an hour. The soaking liquid is used in some recipes, but not in others.

The larger fresh chillies (Anaheim, Poblano) are often toasted over an open flame until the skin is blistered all over; if you don't have an open flame, try 'dry-frying', below, or use a grill (broiler). When they are thoroughly blistered, put them in a plastic bag for twenty minutes to steam. They will then be quite easy to peel.

'Dry-frying' Because ovens and overhead grills (broilers) do not play a large part in traditional Mexican cooking, many things are cooked on a hot, seasoned griddle or frying-pan, without any oil or liquid. Tomatoes are often cooked like this before being added to sauces; garlic is softened this way; nuts and seeds are roasted or toasted; and as already mentioned, chillies are toasted. Grilling (broiling) is an acceptable substitute in many cases.

A roasted and blistered chilli pepper.

13

EATING – MEXICAN STYLE

Mexican eating habits are based, to a large extent, on those of old Spain; and, as in modern Spain, timescales based on a medieval agricultural society are yielding to the pressures of the late twentieth century.

Traditionally, there were four meals a day. The first was a light breakfast (*almuerzo*) of sweet pastries, coffee or chocolate and orange juice; this was eaten quite late, perhaps as late as nine or nine-thirty, for few Mexicans rise early unless they have to. Those who did rise early would have something more substantial – perhaps tacos or enchiladas – at seven or eight.

Second came the substantial *merienda* or 'second breakfast' at ten-thirty or eleven: huevos rancheros, omelettes, even steaks. Then, at around two, the main meal of the day was the *comida*: it might easily run to half a dozen courses, and last a couple of hours, with time for a nap of an hour or two afterward – the famous siesta. *Cena* (supper) was a lighter version of the comida, rarely beginning before nine in the evening and frequently stretching until midnight. All meals, except perhaps almuerzo, were as much social occasions as functional ones: a time to talk, to relax, to enjoy the company of family and friends.

In a world dominated by gringo time-values, even the Mexicans are beginning to modify all this. In a large city,

the family comida is no longer feasible because it would take too long to travel to and from work. Without a good comida, the cena increases in importance, but is likely to be taken a little earlier – perhaps as early as eight o'clock, though most Mexicans would regard the six o'clock meal that is routine for many gringo families as barbarously early, unless they had been working in the fields all day.

Because few readers will be able to adapt their timetable to a traditional Mexican life-style, I have assumed that the dishes in this book will normally be cooked in the evening; the result is inevitably a cross between comida and cena. You may care, though, to try a big comida for family and friends on, say, a Sundy afternoon; invite everyone for about one o'clock, and set aside four or five hours. You will find it very enjoyable . . .

The full sequence of a comida includes *entremés* or appetizers; *sopa* (soup); *pasta* (engagingly translated as 'dry soup'); fish; meat or fowl, with salad; *postre* (dessert); and coffee. For cena, the pasta is usually omitted, and the dishes are often lighter: consommé instead of a hearty soup, sliced cold meat instead of hot, and so forth. The sequence of recipes in this book broadly follows the structure of a comida, with an introductory section on basics (tortillas, sauces, etc) and a final section on drinks.

BELOW: A meal in Huejofzingo; RIGHT: Cactus strewn landscape in Candelaria.

TORTILLAS

The tortilla is to Mexican cooking what the potato is to Northern European or North American cooking: the basic, filling, cheap part of the meal that is served with the vast majority of dishes. Historically, dried corn was boiled with lime to make nixtamal, *which was then ground on a* metate *with a* metalpil *to create masa (corn dough). Today, most people buy their tortillas ready made, though a basic corn tortilla is no more than a mixture of masa harina ('harina' is flour), water and salt.*

CORN TORTILLAS

MAKES ABOUT 1 DOZEN

4 cups/450g/1lb masa harina
1¼ cups/300ml/½pt water
1tsp salt

◆ Work all the ingredients together in a large bowl. If the masa is sticky, it is too wet: add some more masa harina, and work it in. If it breaks up, it is too dry: add some more water slowly. You will not harm the dough by handling it repeatedly – indeed, it seems to improve it – and obviously there is no rising or proving time. Ground dried chillies and even grated hard cheese (similar to Parmesan) may be added to the dough to make flavoured tortillas.

◆ The traditional way to shape tortillas, by slapping a ball of masa from hand to hand until it grows into a flat sheet, is extremely difficult to learn as well as being somewhat time-consuming. A tortilla press is a much easier method – use two plastic bags to stop the tortilla sticking to the press – but if you can't get a tortilla press, just roll out a ball of dough between two plastic bags, using a regular-sized rolling pin. Plastic bags are much less likely to stick than the waxed paper recommended in some books. Corn tortillas can be anything from 3–5 cm (1–2 in) in diameter – these are used for appetizers – to about 15 cm (6 in).

◆ Cook the tortillas on a comal, a round cast-iron or earthenware baking sheet used directly over the fire; a griddle or heavy frying pan will do equally well. Each tortilla is cooked for a couple of minutes on each side; they are done when the edges begin to lift, and they are slightly browned. Given that half a dozen people can easily dispose of a couple of dozen tortillas in one meal, you can see why most people buy their tortillas ready made: a dozen tortillas can be an hour's work, but can be bought quite reasonably at the grocer's store or tortilleria.

◆ The best way to re-heat tortillas is over a direct flame; pat them with damp hands if they are uncomfortably dry. Alternatively, use a microwave; or a comal; or an oven set at about 70–90°C/150–200°F/Gas ¼ or Low, with the tortillas wrapped in paper towels and a damp cloth and aluminium foil around the lot.

◆ To fry tortillas, use 1·2–2·5 cm (½–1 in) of *very* hot oil (corn oil or peanut oil – or lard, for traditionalists), and fry to taste. After 30–60 seconds, the tortillas will be limp and flexible; after two or three minutes, they will be hard and crisp, and are known as tostadas. For home-made corn-chips or tostaditas, cut 10 cm (4 in) tortillas into quarters, and fry them in plenty of oil until they are brown and crisp.

FLOUR TORTILLAS

In Mexico, flour tortillas are significantly more expensive than corn tortillas, and the poorest people rarely eat them. They are, however, firmly integrated into Mexican cookery. They are less often fried than corn tortillas; in particular, no-one ever makes chips out of flour tortillas. For big burritos or tostadas compuestas (tostada salads), flour tortillas are however invaluable. The biggest flour tortillas may be as much as 30 cm (1 ft) in diameter.

◆

MAKES 1 DOZEN

**4 cups/450g/1lb plain (all-purpose) flour
1 tsp salt
1 tsp baking powder
1 tbsp lard
¾ cup/180 ml/6 fl oz cold water**

◆ Mix all the dry ingredients; cut in the lard; add enough water to make a stiff dough. Roll on a lightly floured board, or use plastic bags as for corn tortillas.

TORTILLA PRESS

If you can find them, tortilla presses are not very expensive – and they make it much easier to turn out a dozen tortillas!

BURRITOS

A 'burrito' or 'little donkey' is usually made from a large 30 cm (12 in) flour tortilla. Put the filling in the middle; turn up one end to form a flap, which stops the filling falling out; and roll up. Typical fillings include Carne Asada (page 59); shredded meat, prepared as for Ropa Vieja (page 64); or cheese with refried beans (overleaf). In practice you can fill them with leftover roast meat (or any other leftovers), or even scrambled eggs.

OPPOSITE, LEFT: Buying tortillas in Inchitan; ABOVE, RIGHT: A tortilla press. RIGHT: Enchiladas. An enchilada is yet another variety of rolled tortilla. Soften the tortilla by frying for a few seconds, then roll it around cheese, shredded meat, taco – seasoned minced (ground) beef, or anything else that takes your fancy.

FRIJOLES

Frijoles – beans – are a great staple of Mexican food. The type of bean used varies according to what grows locally: black beans, red beans, white beans, pintos, pinquitos, whatever you like. The first stage is to boil the beans. These servings are for hungry people.

◆

BASIC BEANS

S E R V E S   4 – 6

**2 cups/450g/1lb beans
2 onions, finely chopped
5–10 cloves garlic, chopped
1 bay leaf
2–4 serrano chillies
3 tbsp lard or olive oil
1 tomato, peeled, seeded and chopped
Salt and pepper to taste**

◆ Wash and sort the beans; do not soak them. Cover with cold water and add one of the onions, half the garlic, the bay leaf and the chillies. Cover and bring to the boil. Simmer gently, adding more water as necessary. When the beans begin to wrinkle, add 1 tablespoon of the lard or oil, then continue cooking until the beans are soft. This can take almost all day. When they are soft, add salt to taste; adding salt earlier will toughen them unnecessarily. After adding the salt cook for another half-hour, but without adding more water.

◆ Gently cook the other onion and the other half of the garlic in the rest of the lard or oil, until they are golden; add the tomato, and cook for a couple of minutes more. Into this, mash some of the beans together with their cooking liquid to get a thick, smooth paste – about 3 tablespoons should do it. Return the paste to the bean-pot and thicken the beans with it.

FRIJOLES REFRITOS

(Refried Beans)

S E R V E S   6

**Beans, prepared as in Basic Beans
2 cups/450 g/1 lb lard**

◆ Melt 2 tablespoons of lard in a large, heavy skillet or cast-iron saucepan. Mash the beans, made as above, into this; add them a tablespoon at a time. When the mixture is too 'beany', add more lard; it is easiest to have a glass bowl of it, thoroughly softened, to hand. (Use the microwave to soften it.) You should not need the entire pound of lard, though a Mexican might use this much!

◆ The end result should be thick and fairly dry, and very rich and creamy. If you are worried about cholesterol, use olive oil instead of lard. If you don't want to use either, buy canned beans. Try several varieties: some are much better than others. The best are very good, but they are still not as good as home-made refritos.

BLACK BEAN SOUP

S E R V E S   6

**1 cup/225 g/8 oz black beans
9 cups/2 l/3½ pt water
4 tbsp lard
1 medium onion, chopped
2–4 cloves garlic, chopped
½ tsp crumbled dried red chilli, eg arbol
1 tomato, peeled, de-seeded and chopped
¼ tsp oregano
salt
⅓ cup/75 ml/2½ fl oz sherry**

◆ Wash and sort the beans, but do not soak; cook in the water until almost tender. Melt the lard in a frying pan or skillet. Fry the onion, garlic and chilli until the onion is tender but not browned. Add the tomato; cook for a minute longer. Add the mixture to the beans, together with the oregano and salt to taste. Simmer in a covered pot until the beans are tender.

◆ Push the beans through a sieve or (as a poor second choice), smash them in a food processor. Return to the saucepan and cook for a little longer, adding the sherry two minutes before serving.

OPPOSITE: Refried Beans – Frijoles Refritos.

WHITE BEAN SOUP

S E R V E S   4 – 6

1 cup/225 g/8 oz white beans
Salt
Half a leg of pork, chopped into 2.5 cm/1 in cubes
2 tbsp lard
1 onion, chopped
Half a bell pepper, chopped
100 g/4 oz ham, chopped
2 chorizos
350 g/12 oz Salsa de Jicamate (page 25)

or 1 can tomato sauce
Slice of cabbage to garnish

◆ Soak the beans overnight. Boil, adding water as necessary to keep them covered. After 2 hours (or more), add salt. Boil the cubed pork for about half an hour to an hour, in just enough water to cover.

◆ In a large casserole (or cazuela), melt the lard and fry together the onion, pepper, ham and (skinned) chorizos. When the onion is soft, add the tomato sauce and bring to a boil. Add the beans and pork, both with their cooking liquid, and stir. Garnish with the cabbage and simmer for a couple of hours to thicken and blend.

ARROZ

(Rice)

The blandness of rice is a perfect foil to the strong flavours of rich Mexican food: even food that is poco picante goes well with plain boiled rice.

For a bit more 'zip', white rice is often boiled together with a little chilli powder: one teaspoon of the mild pasilla powder per cup of uncooked rice is a good starting point, and you can adjust quantities and type of chilli powder to suit your own preferences. This is an ideal accompaniment to omelettes, carne asada, pork chops and the like.

'Spanish Rice' or 'Mexican Rice' is an altogether richer and more complex dish. The two important features are that the rice is fried before it is boiled, and that saffron is employed as a flavouring agent.

◆

BASIC SPANISH RICE

SERVES 6

2 medium onions, chopped finely
At least 2 cloves garlic, chopped
At least 2 serrano chillies, chopped (fresh or canned)
450 g/1 lb peeled and de-seeded tomatoes
OR 1 can tomatoes
¼ cup/60 ml/2 fl oz olive oil
2 cups/450 g/1 lb rice
¼ tsp whole cumin seed
¼ tsp saffron
4 cups/scant 1 l/32 fl oz chicken stock
Salt and pepper
1 cup/200 g/6 oz peas, fresh or frozen

◆ Purée the onion, garlic, serranos and tomatoes in a blender.

◆ Heat the oil in a large, heavy skillet and fry the rice, stirring frequently, until it is golden. Add the tomato mixture, the spices and the chicken stock; bring to the boil, stirring frequently. When the rice has absorbed all the visible liquid (10–20 minutes), add the peas; stir briefly; then cover tightly and simmer over a very low heat for another 20 minutes or so.

ARROZ CON POLLO

(Chicken with Rice)

SERVES 4

1 1.5 kg/3½–4 lb chicken
Basic Spanish Rice ingredients, as on left

◆ Cut the chicken into serving pieces. Fry until golden; drain and set aside. In the same oil, fry the chopped or sliced onion together with the garlic. Drain, and add to the chicken, together with the tomatoes, stock and spices. Bring to the boil; simmer for about half an hour.

◆ Meanwhile, still in the same oil – adding a little more if necessary – fry the rice until it is golden, stirring frequently. Add the rice to the chicken; mix well; bring back to the boil; and proceed as for Basic Spanish Rice, above. You can omit the peas.

PAELLA

SERVES 4 – 6

◆ Instead of – or in addition to – chicken or other poultry, paella contains some or all of the following: shrimps or prawns (whole or shelled); clams, oysters or other bivalves; conch or snail; pork, cut up finely; small crabs; crayfish; chunks of fish; and whatever else you like. Everything is added to the fried rice, along with the broth, and cooked fairly slowly. You need to cover and uncover the dish from time to time, in order to stop it drying out on the one hand or becoming excessively soupy on the other.

OPPOSITE, LEFT: Paella;
ABOVE: Arroz con Pollo;
RIGHT: Guitar players in Mexico
City.

SALSA

'Salsa' literally means 'sauce', but in the absence of other qualifications it normally means salsa cruda, 'raw sauce', which appears on the table as regularly as pepper and salt. It is frequently used as a dip, with corn chips, but it can be spooned on to almost any savoury dish: omelettes, chiles rellenos, meat . . . you name it. Most salsas crudas improve and mature (grow hotter!) if left overnight in the refrigerator. The basic ingredients, mixed-and-matched in a wide variety of combinations, are dried or fresh peppers; onions; tomatoes (including tomatillos); garlic, and cilantro (coriander). Optional additions include oregano, vinegar and olive oil.

◆

FRESH SALSA

**Small handful of coriander
leaves
1 large onion, red or white
1 650 g/24 oz can tomatoes
1—4 cloves garlic
2 serrano chillies, or 1 jalapeno**

◆ Wash the coriander and remove the coarser stems and roots. A gringo might use as little as a teaspoon of chopped coriander; a Mexican would probably use half a bunch – about a handful, before chopping.

◆ Chop the onion and tomatoes finely, the garlic, chilli pepper and coriander very finely. Put them all in a large bowl. Squish them together with your hand, squeezing and rubbing to blend and increase flavour.

◆ You can also use a food processor. Chop the garlic and pepper first; then add the onion, and chop some more; then add the rest. The traditional way to make it is to grind the ingredients together in a pestle and mortar.

SALSA VARIATIONS

▶ Roast one or two Poblano or Anaheim chillies over an open flame; when they are charred all over, remove the skin. Remove the seeds and veins; chop; add to the salsa.

▶ Use fresh tomatoes instead of canned: either peel them (dip in boiling water for 10–30 seconds) or leave the skins on. Remove the tomato seeds, or not, as you feel inclined.

▶ For a thicker salsa, use a can of crushed tomatoes with added tomato purée (paste).

▶ If you like, add any of the following: a pinch of oregano; and/or a tablespoon of wine vinegar or lime juice; and/or a tablespoon of olive oil.

▶ Fresh coriander seeds are a wonderful addition to salsa – a strong argument for growing your own.

▶ In the absence of fresh serrano chillies, shred a red chilli and grind it in a little water with the garlic; leave to soak for a while; and add this paste to the tomato, onion and coriander.

▶ For a rock-bottom-basic dipping salsa, add the same chilli/garlic paste to half a can of commercial tomato sauce.

SALSA VERDE

(Green Salsa)

Salsa verde is also uncooked, but it is (usually) hotter than salsa cruda. It is a good way of adding flavour to dull, bulky foods if you are poor, but it has a place on the rich man's table, too. If you use it as a dip, don't scoop out large quantities: this stuff is hot.

◆

MAKES 2 CUPS

**1 300 g/10 oz can tomatillos
1 small white onion
2—4 serrano chillies
2—4 cloves garlic
1 tbsp chopped fresh coriander**

◆ Smash the lot together in a food processor – this is a fine-grained sauce. Alternatively, chop finely; mash together; and grind in a pestle and mortar.

◆ If you are using fresh tomatillos, remove the dry outer husk, but *don't* be tempted to skin or seed them – there will be nothing left. You can increase the cilantro (coriander) as much as you like. A really basic salsa verde consists only of tomatillos, chilli peppers and coriander.

GUACAMOLE

The third great dip/sauce/garnish, after salsa cruda and salsa verde, is guacamole. At its simplest, this is no more than mashed avocado, but each person has his or her own views on what improves mashed avocado. When you make guacamole, make plenty: it is so delicious that a couple of mouthfuls is more tantalizing than satisfying. If avocados are too expensive, either grit your teeth and pay the money, or leave it until another time. The recipe below is (just) enough for four, served with corn chips.

◆

BASIC GUACAMOLE

S E R V E S 4

½ dried red chilli, preferably arbol
1 clove garlic
2 large or 4 small avocados, very ripe

◆ Seed and shred the chilli pepper; pound in a mortar with the garlic and a tablespoon or two of water. Leave for 5–10 minutes. Mash the avocado with an old-fashioned wooden potato masher. Mix in the chilli/garlic paste, strained through a tea-strainer. This is good for a dip; for a garnish, you can double the amounts of garlic and pepper.

FANCY GUACAMOLE

S E R V E S 4

Basic ingredients, as above
1 medium tomato
½ small white onion
1 tbsp chopped coriander
Salt

◆ Peel, seed, and finely chop the tomato. Chop the onion finely in a food processor. Add these ingredients to the guacamole. Salt to taste – the basic recipe really does not need salt.

◆ For further variations, omit the red pepper or the garlic or both, and add one finely chopped serrano. You may also wish to add chopped coriander. None of this will necessarily make a better guacamole than the other, just different.

OPPOSITE: Carnaditas con Salsa Verde; ABOVE, RIGHT: Guacamole; LEFT: Garlic on sale in Toluca market.

COOKED SALSAS

The two basic cooked salsas are salsa de jicamate (tomato salsa) and mole verde (green or tomatillo sauce). Both may be bought ready-made in cans, but they are not that difficult to make, and they do taste much better than the canned variety. If you must use canned tomato sauce, at least fry a little onion and garlic in olive oil until soft, and add the commercial stuff to that. One small onion and a clove or two of garlic per can will improve canned sauce no end – but still won't match the real thing.

♦

SALSA DI JICAMATE

(Basic Tomato Sauce)

MAKES EQUIVALENT OF
3 STANDARD CANS

1 650 g/24 oz can tomatoes, chopped
1 170 g/6 oz can tomato purée (paste)
2 large onions, finely chopped
5–10 cloves garlic
2–4 serrano chillies
1 glass/200 ml/6 fl oz red wine or sherry
Pinch each parsley, sage, rosemary, thyme, oregano
Salt and pepper to taste
Olive oil for frying
Sugar if necessary
Coriander

♦ In two or three tablespoons of oil, fry the onions and garlic. When they are soft and golden, add the serranos, tomatoes, tomato purée (paste), wine, spices and seasoning. Add sugar if the sauce is too sharp; this will depend on the wine and the tomatoes, and often you won't need sugar. Simmer for 15–30 minutes; add the coriander a minute or two before the end of cooking.

♦ You can omit the wine; if you do, omit the tomato purée as well.

OPPOSITE: Fresh ingredients in Toluca market; INSET: Pork and Chicken in Mole Verde.

MOLE VERDE

(Green Sauce)

MAKES EQUIVALENT OF
2–3 STANDARD CANS

1 300 g/10oz can tomatillos
5 large fresh chillies (Anaheim or poblano)
¼ cup/60 g/2 oz chopped onion
3 corn tortillas, torn into small pieces
1–4 cloves garlic
100 g/4 oz spinach, fresh or frozen (optional)
3 cups/750 ml/24 fl oz chicken stock

♦ Prepare the chillies as described on pages 12–13. Peel; remove seeds and veins; chop coarsely.

♦ Drain the tomatillos. Add them to the other ingredients, except the stock, in a blender; purée. You may need to do this in batches unless you have a very large blender.

♦ Mix the blended purée with the sauce. Simmer the mixture for about an hour. Season to taste; add more stock if the sauce is too thick.

PORK AND CHICKEN IN MOLE VERDE

SERVES 4 – 6

1.5 kg/2–3 lb pork
1 kg/1–2 lb chicken drumsticks
1 recipe Green Sauce, as above

♦ Country-style ribs are a good choice for this: allow one big slice per person, with perhaps one spare. Alternatively, use any reasonably lean pork, cut into cubes about two inches (5 cm) on a side. You can of course use any other meat, though pork and chicken together are particularly good.

♦ Boil the meat until it is very tender indeed, at least an hour: two hours is not too much. If you use ribs, the meat should be falling off the bone. Once it is cooked, fry it briefly in oil to give an attractive brown finish – though this step is more cosmetic than culinary.

♦ Cover the meat with the sauce, and heat in a cool oven under 100°C/200°F/Gas ¼, for an hour or more. The important thing is to warm the ingredients through, and blend the flavours, without burning the sauce. This dish is perfect for freezing and re-heating later.

OTHER SAUCES

There are several other vinegar-based sauces that are a cross between salsa and chutneys. They are used as marinading pastes; or diluted with more vinegar, as in fish in escabeche; or simply served as a side dish. Of the three recipes given here, adobo sauce is the most time-consuming to make, but it lasts for a very long time: it will keep for months in the refrigerator. By the time you need more, you have forgotten how much trouble it was to make, and the memory of that delightful flavour lingers on.

◆

ADOBO SAUCE

M A K E S   ½   C U P

4 medium dried anchos chillies (60 g/2 oz)
6 medium dried guajillos chillies (45 g/1½ oz)
8 cloves garlic, unpeeled
10 black peppercorns
10–15 mm/½ in cinnamon bark
2 large bay leaves, torn up
½ tsp dried oregano
½ tsp dried thyme
3 tbsp wine or cider vinegar
2 whole cloves
Large pinch cumin seeds
1–2 tsp salt

◆ Prepare the dried chillies as described on page 15 – toasted and soaked. If you can't get guajillos, use all anchos or even pasillas. California or New Mexico chillies will, however, give a much lighter flavour.
◆ 'Dry-fry' the unpeeled garlic in a heavy frying pan with no oil. Turn frequently. After 10–15 minutes, the garlic will be very soft and the blackened, blistered skins can be easily removed – let the cloves cool down before you try!
◆ Grind the cinnamon, cloves, peppercorns, bay leaves and cumin in a pestle and mortar or spice-grinder. The aroma of fresh-ground spices is incomparably superior to ready-ground spices.
◆ Drain the chillies, and put them in a blender with the peeled garlic, the herbs and spices, the vinegar, and a very little water – a couple of tablespoons.
◆ Now comes the tedious part. Blend this mixture to a smooth paste. You will need to stop every few seconds, and push the mixture down on to the blades; you may even need to add another tablespoon of water. *Don't* add too much water, though, or the sauce will be weak and watery. It can easily take five or ten minutes to get a reasonably

smooth paste, but at least it's easier than doing it the traditional way, with a coarse-grained pestle and mortar.
◆ Finally, strain the sauce through a stainless-steel mesh: this is also tedious, as it takes a long time. The easiest way to do it is to use the pestle inside the strainer. You will be left with a smooth, creamy paste and a mass of pungent pulp. Discard the pulp; keep the paste in the refrigerator in a glass jar with a plastic top, as it will corrode metal ferociously.

PUERCO ADOBADO

◆ Smear adobo sauce thickly on pork chops.
◆ Marinate them overnight (in a plastic bag, for convenience).
◆ Fry, grill (broil) or barbecue next day.

RECADO DE BISTECK

This is rather easier to make than adobo. Despite the name, it is used for many things other than beefsteak (bisteck): for example, it makes an excellent sauce for fish in escabeche (see page 54), and it is very good spread on a beef roast and left overnight. If you are going to go to the trouble of making it, use whole spices: pre-ground spices have far less flavour and aroma.

◆

M A K E S   ½   C U P

24 cloves garlic
2 tsp black peppercorns
½ tsp allspice berries
½ tsp whole cloves
½ tsp cumin seeds
1 tbsp dried oregano
1 tsp salt
2 tbsp wine or cider vinegar
1 tsp flour

◆ 'Dry-fry' the unpeeled garlic as for adobo sauce.
◆ Grind together the black pepper, allspice, cloves, cumin and oregano.
◆ Peel the garlic, chop finely, and then in a large pestle and mortar mash the garlic and the spices together. When they are thoroughly combined, work in the vinegar and flour. Leave overnight in a covered glass jar to allow the flavours to combine.

ABOVE: Ingredients for Adobo Sauce; BELOW: Puerco Adobado.

ESCABECHE

MAKES 3 CUPS

6 pickled wax peppers, sliced and de-seeded
2 large bell peppers, sliced, de-seeded
and de-veined
2 large white onions, sliced
2 or more cloves garlic, finely chopped
2 cups/450 ml/16 fl oz vinegar
1 tsp saltt
$\frac{1}{2}$ tsp oregano
2 bay leaves
$\frac{1}{4}$ tsp freshly ground black pepper
Pinch cumin

◆ Fry the peppers, onion and garlic together until they are soft. Add all the other ingredients, and bring to a boil. As soon as it starts to boil, remove it from the heat and set it aside to cool. This is a typical escabeche for fish: for meat or poultry, reduce the oil to two tablespoons.

APPETIZERS AND SNACKS

The distinctions between an appetizer, a snack and a light meal are blurred; many of the dishes here can be any or all of these, or even (if served in sufficient quantities) a main course. Queso Fundido is a typical starter in Mexican restaurants in Mexico; Chili con Queso is a dip; and Quesadillas are more of a snack.

◆

BASIC QUESO FUNDIDO

◆ For an individual or two-person serving, heat a small ovenproof serving dish at about 200°C/375°F/Gas 5 in the oven. When it is hot, fill it with cubes of cheese (Jack cheese is ideal; Cheddar will do) and return it to the oven for 5–10 minutes, until the cheese is completely melted. Serve with hot flour tortillas and Salsa Cruda. For a touch of luxury, add a shot or two of brandy to the cheese before it begins to melt.

CHILI CON QUESO

S E R V E S 2

1 medium onion, finely chopped
2 tbsp/30 g/1 oz butter
250 g/8 oz canned tomatoes, chopped
1–3 serrano chillies
3 cups grated (shredded) Jack or Cheddar cheese
$\frac{1}{2}$ cup/120 ml/4 fl oz sour cream (optional)

◆ Fry the onion gently in the butter until it is translucent. Add the tomatoes and chilli peppers; simmer, stirring frequently, until thickened. Add the cheese, stirring as you do. Cook, stirring constantly, until the cheese melts. For a thinner dip, add the cream.

ABOVE, LEFT: Scene in Inchitan; ABOVE, RIGHT: Chilie con Queso; OPPOSITE: Quesadillas Sincronizadas.

QUESADILLAS

Quesadillas are a very simple, very economical, and surprisingly filling and delicious snack. They consist of nothing more than tortillas with a melted cheese filling. The best cheese is Oaxaca, but Jack and mozarella are fine, and Cheddar will do.

◆

◆ The usual way to make them is to fry a tortilla in an almost dry pan (or on a griddle) until it is soft; flip it over; put a lump or a handful of grated (shredded) cheese in the middle; fold it in half; and continue to cook it, turning it over occasionally, until the cheese melts.

◆ Quesadillas Sincronizadas, or 'synchronized quesadillas' are made as shown, with two quesadillas stuck together with melted cheese; they are quartered for serving.

◆ If you are making quesadillas with uncooked tortillas, you can pinch together the edges of a basic turnover quesadilla and fry the whole thing in deep fat.

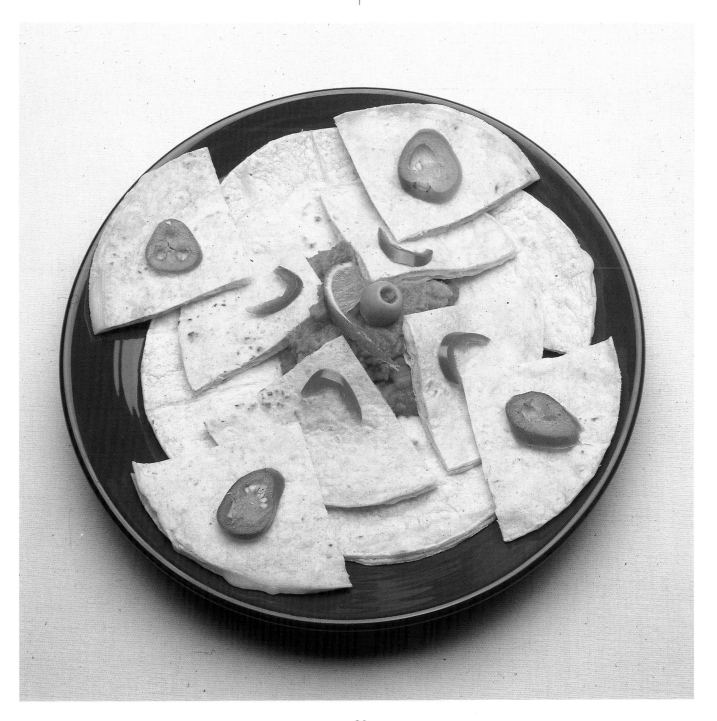

29

EMPANADAS

Empanadas are little turnovers that may contain sweet or savory ingredients. As so often, you can use both your imagination and your leftovers to the full; this is a basic savory empanada.

◆

S E R V E S 4

500 g/1 lb shortcrust pastry
250 g/½ lb minced (ground) beef
1 medium onion
1 small bell pepper, red or green
2 medium tomatoes
1 tablespoon seedless white raisins
1 dried red chilli (arbol or similar)
½ teaspoon cumin seed
2 tablespoons olive oil
Pepper and salt

◆ Skin, seed and chop the tomatoes. Remove the seeds and veins from the bell pepper; chop. Chop the onion finely. Fry these ingredients together in the oil, and fry until soft. Add the beef; fry until the meat is brown and crumbly.

◆ Crumble the dried pepper. Use the cumin seeds whole, or for still better flavour, crush them using a pestle and mortar. Add the dried pepper, cumin and raisins to the mixture in the skillet. Season to taste, and cook for another ten minutes or so. Set aside to cool.

◆ Roll the dough into five-inch (12-cm) rounds; you should get about eight. Divide the filling equally between them, placing it on one half of the round and folding over to seal. Overfilling will make cooking difficult!

◆ Cook in a pre-heated oven at 375°F/190°C until the pastry is golden brown – about 35 minutes. Serve hot. Some people prefer to deep-fry their empanadas.

TOSTADAS

The huge bowl-shaped 'tostadas grandes', made from a deep-fried tortilla and filled with all kinds of meat, beans, salad and so forth are not very Mexican. The true Mexican tostada compuesta *is made with much the same ingredients, but is smaller and simpler. Typically, a tostada would form one course of a long* comida, *but it would not be unusual to order a couple for* merienda.
You can use almost any toppings, as usual: this one uses chicken and sour cream in addition to the standard beans-and-salad.

◆

CHICKEN TOSTADA

S E R V E S 6

Six regular-size tortillas
Oil or lard for frying
One small skinned, boneless chicken breast
Half a lettuce
Three tomatoes
2 cups/500 g/1 lb refried beans
¼ cup/100 ml/4 oz sour cream
Garnishes (optional): see below

◆ Boil the chicken breast until it is soft enough to be shredded with two forks – anything up to an hour. Shred.

◆ Fry the tortillas in the oil or lard until crisp – or use ready-made 'tostada shells'.

◆ Top the tostada shells with a generous layer of beans, about 2–3 tablespoons per tortilla. On top of this, place one-sixth of the shredded chicken. Next, add the shredded lettuce; sliced tomato; and sour cream. Optional garnishes include sliced red or green (spring) onions; slices of avocado; olives; and (for colour, as here) a pinch of paprika.

ABOVE: Empanadas.   OPPOSITE: Making tortillas in Toluca market.
LEFT: Tostadas.

HUEVOS

(Eggs)

In addition to their use in many other dishes, eggs form the basis of a number of hearty dishes for the merienda *or 'second breakfast'. You may care to try them for brunch.*

◆

HUEVOS RANCHEROS

(Ranch-style Eggs)

'Ranch-style eggs' vary widely in quality and quantity if you order them in a restaurant; in Baja California, they may even make it with scrambled eggs. The basic recipe, per person, is as follows:

◆

S E R V E S   1

2 small (100 mm/4 in) tortillas
2 eggs
Lard for frying
Salsa Ranchera (below) or other salsa
Refritos (refried beans)

◆ If you do not have small tortillas, cut circles from larger ones: a sharp-edged bowl makes a good cookie-cutter, or cut around a cup with a knife.

◆ Fry the tortillas. Some like them just limp; others prefer them crispy. Put them side by side on a plate; put the fried eggs on top 'sunny-side up'. Pour salsa over the top, and serve the beans alongside.
◆ Alternatively, place the beans on the tortillas, and put the eggs on top of the beans.

SALSA RANCHERA

2 tbsp olive oil
½ can tomatoes, drained and mashed
Sugar if necessary
2–4 jalapeno chillies, sliced
1 tbsp wine vinegar
Salt and pepper to taste

◆ In the olive oil, fry the tomatoes to a thick purée; season, adding sugar if the sauce is too sharp. Remove from the heat, add the chopped chillies and vinegar, and mix well. Leave to mature overnight in the refrigerator.

TORTILLA DE HUEVO

This has nothing to do with a regular Mexican tortilla; it's a Mexican omelette. This is the basic recipe: add shrimp, diced chicken, etc, according to taste and budget, and garnish with avocado or guacamole.

◆

S E R V E S   2

2 whole spring (green) onions, chopped
2 serrano chillies, finely chopped
2 tbsp lard or butter for frying
1 small tomato, chopped
8 eggs
4 tbsp water
Salt and pepper to taste

◆ Fry the onions and chillies together, until golden. Add the tomato; cook and reduce for 3–5 minutes, stirring occasionally.
◆ Beat the eggs with water. Stir into the pan with the onion-chilli-tomato mixture. Cook over a low heat until set; fold in half to serve.

LEFT: Huevos Rancheros; OPPOSITE: Tartahumara Indians in Chihuahua.

HUEVOS REVUELTOS

(Scrambled Eggs)

Mexicans are very fond of scrambling eggs with meat: a little chorizo, perhaps, or some ham, or even machomo, for which the recipe is given below. The following makes a memorable brunch for four. (The champagne is not essential, but it goes uniquely well with heavy, rich huevos revueltos.)

◆

SERVES 4

15 eggs
Salt and pepper
¼ cup/60 g/2 oz butter
1 can (or equivalent) refried beans
Shredded lettuce and other salad garnish
Flour tortillas
1 bottle champagne

◆ Beat the eggs well, and season with pepper and salt to taste.
◆ For plain scrambled eggs, melt the butter over a very low heat and stir in the eggs: they should cook to a creamy, rather than a chewy, consistency.
◆ Serve with beans, a salad garnish and tortillas . . . and champagne.

VARIATIONS

1 or 2 sliced fresh or pickled jalapeno peppers
About 150 g/4–6 oz ham
About 200 g/6–8 oz chorizo
About 150 g/4–6 oz smoked fish
One handful machomo (see below)

▶ For chorizo, use only about a quarter as much butter. Skin and chop the sausage, and fry: it will release more than enough fat to scramble the eggs. Reduce the heat, add the eggs (and peppers, if you like) and stir until set. This will not be creamy.
▶ For ham, use the full amount of butter. Cut sliced ham in strips: dice thicker pieces of ham. Fry for 30 seconds over a low heat; add the eggs; stir until set. You can make this one creamy or chewy, as you like. Again, peppers are optional.
▶ With smoked fish, a creamy consistency is more desirable. Add the flaked or diced fish after the eggs: do not fry beforehand.

▶ If you are using machomo, increase the amount of butter by 50 to 100 per cent, and add the machomo and eggs simultaneously. Machaca tastes very similar to machomo, but is made from dried meat rather than fish.

MACHOMO

In addition to its use with eggs, machomo makes a good filling for tacos or burritos. It keeps for several days in a plastic bag in the refrigerator.

◆

MAKES 200–300 g/8–12 oz

450 g/1 lb beef
2 cloves garlic
6 peppercorns
1 clove
1 bay leaf
2 small onions
1 tbsp lard

◆ Chop the beef into approx. 5 cm (2 in) cubes. Put in a saucepan with just enough water to cover. Add all the other ingredients except one of the small onions and the lard. Bring to the boil and simmer until the beef is soft enough to be shredded with two forks.
◆ Strain off the stock and save it for use in another recipe; discard the onion, garlic, etc.
◆ Shred the beef as finely as possible. Chop the onion finely. Melt the lard in a skillet or frying pan, and fry the onion until it is light golden. Add the shredded beef, and continue to fry, stirring constantly. Slowly, the beef will begin to dry out. When it is crisp, or at least very dry, the machomo is ready: this takes about ten minutes.

OPPOSITE: Machomo.

CHILES RELLENOS

(Stuffed Peppers)

The classic Mexican way of preparing chiles rellenos is absolutely nothing like the Spanish dish of the same name. The peppers are Anaheim or poblano chillies, not bell peppers; they are stuffed with cheese, not with a rice-meat mixture; and they are coated in egg and deep-fried instead of being baked in the oven. Four people can easily put away a dozen as a main course, and they are rather time-consuming to make if you use fresh chillies. On the other hand, canned chillies will not be anything like as good as fresh ones: use them only if you are desperate for time. Until you've had the real thing, you don't know what you're missing.

◆

S E R V E S 4

12 Anaheim or Poblano chillies
450 g/1 lb Cheddar or Jack cheese
1 cup/100 g/4 oz plain (all-purpose) flour
6 eggs
Oil or lard for frying

◆ Roast and skin the chillies as described on page 15. Slitting open the side of the chilli, remove the seeds and veins, but be careful not to break the flesh. Into each chilli, insert a piece of cheese 'stuffing'; taper the end of the cheese slightly, if necessary. Roll the peeled, de-seeded, stuffed chillies in flour.

◆ Beat the egg yolks and whites separately; the whites should be beaten to the stiff peak stage. Re-combine the eggs and beat together quickly.

◆ Dip the chillies in the egg batter; be sure to cover the whole surface evenly. Fry in fat or oil that is more than 3 cm (1 in) deep. Keep them warm in the oven until they are ready to serve.

◆ Serve with refried beans and basic spiced rice, or fancier rice if you feel like it.

36

STUFFED BELL PEPPERS

This, the New World version of chiles rellenos made with bell peppers, rice and meat is also popular in the Old World.

◆

S E R V E S   4

3 rashers bacon, finely chopped
1 tbsp olive oil
1 small onion, chopped
225 g/½ lb minced (ground) beef
2 cups/450 g/1 lb leftover Mexican rice (cooked)
4 very large green bell peppers

◆ Fry the bacon in a little oil; in the bacon fat, fry the onion and beef. When the beef is cooked, add the rice. Warm through.

◆ Cut the tops off the peppers. Remove the seeds and veins. Stuff the beef-bacon-rice mixture into the peppers. (Let it mound over the top if need be.) Bake in a moderately hot oven 200°C/375°F/Gas 5 until the peppers are cooked – about 30–40 minutes.

O P P O S I T E : Chiles Rellenos; A B O V E : Stuffed Bell Peppers; B E L O W : Oaxaca.

37

MEAT APPETIZERS

The sheer quantity of meat in some Mexican dishes amazes some people. These two appetizers are definitely for carnivores!

◆

ALBONDIGUITAS

The meatballs that make up the famous Albondigas Soup (page 46) are prepared in a number of other ways. If they are deep-fried, they can be served on their own as a snack or as a meat dish; or with a tomato sauce; or even in a boleta (Mexican roll) to make a torta, the Mexican equivalent of the American 'submarine' sandwich. If you don't mind a little culture shock, they are also excellent in spaghetti sauce . . .

◆

SERVES 12

**450 g/1 lb lean minced (ground) beef
350 g/12 oz minced (ground) pork
½ cup/120 g/4 oz cooked rice
1 small onion, chopped very finely
2 cloves garlic, chopped very finely
2 eggs
Chopped coriander (optional)
Salt and pepper to taste
Lard or oil for frying**

◆ Mix everything together thoroughly. Form the mixture into balls: for a main course, rather smaller than a golf-ball, for appetizers (albondiguitas), about 2–3 cm (1 in) in diameter. Mexican cooks often insert a piece of hard-boiled egg or half an olive in the middle.

◆ Deep-fry for several minutes – it takes a while for the centre to be cooked fully. As an appetizer, serve on tooth-picks. For a main course, serve with tomato sauce (page 26). You can either fry the meatballs first, or poach them in the sauce.

CARNITAS

Carnitas or 'little meats' are a popular snack, but need a certain amount of confidence (and a heavy iron pan) if they are to be prepared successfully. You can use any cheap cuts of pork; in fact, you have to use cheap, fatty meat or the dish will not cook properly.

◆

SERVES 12

**1.5 kg/3 lb boned, skinned pork shoulder
Salt to taste (try 2 tsp)**

◆ Cut the meat into pieces about 5 × 2 × 2 cm (2 × ¾ × ¾ in). Put in a heavy flameproof casserole or Dutch oven, with just enough water to cover the meat. Bring it to the boil.

◆ Reduce the heat, but keep the pot boiling: leave it uncovered. By the time all the water has evaporated – half an hour or so – the meat should be cooked but not falling apart. Then, lower the heat again, and allow the fat to render out. Turn frequently; the carnitas are ready when they are browned all over. This takes another hour to an hour and a half.

OPPOSITE: Black pottery in Oaxaca; RIGHT: Albondiguitas.

LEFT: Ensalada de Col; BELOW: Pico de Gallo; OPPOSITE: Papaya growing in Yucatan.

SALADS

◆◆◆◆◆◆◆◆◆◆◆◆◆◆

Salads are not a particularly Mexican art-form: the famous Caesar Salad seems to have been invented primarily for gringos, and most Mexicans get their greenery as part of their regular diet: many Mexican dishes are garnished with salad, and while some recipes are almost pure meat, others contain vegetables. If you want to serve a salad, these are probably the most Mexican.

ENSALADA DE COL

(Cabbage Salad)

S E R V E S 4

½ head cabbage, shredded
1 or more avocados, diced
1 or more tomatoes, sliced
1 red onion, thinly sliced
2 sticks celery, chopped
1 small jicama, diced or sliced
1 small handful raisins
1 small handful walnuts or almonds
1 medium carrot, shredded
1 cooked beet, sliced
1 handful coriander leaves, chopped
100 g/4 oz cheese, diced

◆ Mix the cabbage with any or all of the above. Make a vinaigrette-type dressing, but use lime juice (or half-and-half lime juice and wine vinegar) with the olive oil, instead of just vinegar. Use two parts of olive oil to one part lime juice, and add a pinch of dry mustard to help the dressing emulsify when you shake it.

PICO DE GALLO

When made as illustrated, with the ingredients coarsely chopped, this is an excellent snack or side-salad. Chop the ingredients more finely and you have a salsa. 'Pico de gallo' means 'rooster's bill'; the idea is that you pick at this salad the way a rooster picks at the ground.

◆

S E R V E S 4 – 6

1 medium-to-large jicama
2 medium-to-large oranges
Juice of 1 large lemon or 2 limes
Bottled hot sauce

◆ Peel and slice (or chip or dice) the jicama. Peel and slice (or dice) the oranges. Mix, in a bowl, with the lemon or lime juice. Sprinkle with hot sauce – it brings out the flavours of the other ingredients.

◆ Some people add cantaloupes, apples and fresh chopped coriander. Others add lots of salt. Some use tangerines instead of oranges. Whether any of these improve the basic recipe is disputable, but *no hay reglas fijas*.

ENSALADA DE NOPALITOS

Nopalitos are new, young cactus shoots. Fresh, they have a very 'green' taste; cooked, they taste more like green beans. In fact, you can substitute green beans in the likely event that you can't get even canned nopalitos.

◆

S E R V E S 4 – 6

450 g/1 lb nopalitos
(2 small cans, if you must)
2 medium tomatoes, peeled, de-seeded and chopped
½ small onion, finely chopped
Large pinch oregano
3 tbsp olive oil
2 tbsp red wine vinegar
½–1 tbsp chopped coriander
Salt and pepper

◆ Toss all the ingredients together. Serve on a bed of lettuce leaves (preferably Romaine), garnished with crumbled fresh cheese, and a small onion and a tomato, both sliced very thinly. Strips of pickled jalapenos (with the seeds removed) will add zest: use jalapenos en escabeche if you can get them.

VEGETABLES

Like salads, vegetables are not considered as a separate part of Mexican cooking; they are just there, *mixed with the meat or fish or whatever. There are, however, a couple of Mexican vegetable dishes that are worth knowing about.*

◆

COLACHE

This is a mixture of whatever vegetables happen to be in season. Some are boiled before they are fried; others are fried from raw. This is a typical mixture – the colache illustrated also contains a quarter of a small pumpkin, because it was made just before Hallowe'en.

BELOW: Colache; OPPOSITE: Church in Tehnantepec.

SERVES 4 – 6

450 g/1 lb courgettes (zucchini)
1 cup/250 g/8 oz cooked hominy (use canned)
1 cup/250 g/8 oz cooked green beans
(or use canned)
1 cup/250 ml/8 fl oz olive oil or lard
1 small onion, chopped
1 ear corn, quartered as shown
3 fresh tomatoes, peeled
Salt

◆ Parboil the courgettes whole: they should still be firm, rather than soft. Slice. Drain the hominy and beans.
◆ In the oil or lard, cook the onion gently into translucent. Add the other ingredients. Season to taste; simmer, loosely covered (leave the lid askew) for 10 minutes, stirring occasionally. (The parboiled pumpkin was added just before serving; otherwise, it would have disintegrated.)

42

LEGUMBRES ASADOS

(Barbecued Vegetables)

Instead of being boiled, some vegetables are cooked over a dry heat: a barbecue, or even a hot griddle or comal. Two that are particularly successful like this are cebollos (or cebollitos) asados and elote asado.
Cebollitos are spring onions, green onions, ciboes, chipples – call them what you will – the long, thin onions that are normally chopped and used as a garnish. Just grill them over charcoal until they are a rich golden colour; they will lose their oniony 'tang' and become surprisingly sweet.
Elotes are ears of corn. Before grilling, and at intervals during grilling, they are normally dipped in brine: dip two or three times in the five minutes or so that they are cooking, and turn the ears constantly. Use sea-water, or 100 g/4 oz of salt in 4 cups/1 litre/1½ pt of water. This is the 'parched corn' that was adopted by both Yankees and Rebels in the War Between the States.

SOUPS

Mexicans recognize two distinct kinds of soup: the usual variety, and 'sopas secas' or 'dry soups'. A 'dry soup', also known as 'pasta', is so called because it incorporates a dry ingredient (rice, tortillas, pasta) which soaks up some or all of the liquid. At a comida, both should be served, the sopa seca second.

◆

CALDO TLALPENO

About the only constant things in Caldo Tlalpeno (Tlalpen-style soup) are chicken and avocado. Sometimes the soup is made with a chicken stock; sometimes with vegetable stock. Usually (but not invariably) it contains some kind of chilli pepper, though which sort of pepper varies widely. Gringo versions usually contain little or no garlic; Mexican versions may contain a whole head. This is a simple, authentic version, for four modest servings.

◆

S E R V E S 4

100 g/4 oz chicken (white meat)
4 cups/1 l/1½ pt chicken stock
1 or 2 dried red chillies (chili arbole)
1–5 cloves garlic
3 tbsp water
Salt to taste (½–1 tsp)
1 avocado
Coriander to garnish (about half a handful)

◆ Slice the chicken into julienne strips. If the chicken is not cooked, bring the chicken stock to a boil; simmer the meat until it is cooked (less than 5 minutes). Otherwise, bring the stock and chicken to a simmering boil. Doubling the amount of chicken will not do any harm.

◆ De-seed the chillies; tear into pieces; grind in a pestle and mortar with the garlic and 3 tablespoons of water. Strain into the stock. Stir, simmer for a couple of minutes, and add salt to taste.

◆ Peel the avocado and slice into strips. Separate the slices carefully before dropping them into the soup, or they will stick together. They will sink for a few moments, then float to the surface. When they do, the soup is ready. Chop some coriander and float it on the surface for a garnish.

SOPA DE AJO

(Garlic Soup)

Because the garlic is first fried, then boiled in the soup, this does not taste anything like as overpowering as most people expect. In fact, it is a very delicate soup. This is for four modest servings.

◆

S E R V E S 4

10 cloves garlic
½ tsp flour
2 tbsp butter
4 cups/1 l/1½ pt beef or chicken stock
Hot sauce (Tabasco), salt and pepper
4 eggs
Croûtons or well-browned toast (optional)
2 tbsp crumbled cheese to garnish
1 tbsp chopped parsley to garnish

◆ Chop the garlic as finely as possible, then mash. Add the flour, and fry gently in butter. When it is translucent, add the stock; bring to the boil and simmer for 15 minutes. Strain through a fine-mesh sieve; season with pepper, salt and hot sauce (a few drops is all you need).

◆ Return to the fire. With the soup at a gentle boil, slip in the eggs and poach them. When they are firm, the soup is done. Serve over croûtons or toast; garnish with crumbled cheese and chopped parsley.

V A R I A T I O N S

Instead of serving the soup in the usual way, in a tureen, try this:

▶ Heat four individual serving bowls in the oven at about 120°C/250°F)Gas ½. Pour the boiling soup into these, and add the egg *yolk* only. Let stand for a couple of minutes, preferably covered, and serve. The yolk will still be liquid, but this is quite normal in Mexico. Add the croûtons with the garnish, or omit them.

▶ Yet another variation calls for using a fried egg. Fry the egg lightly in olive oil, and slide on to the soup, 'sunny-side up'. The croûtons are useful here to support the egg.

OPPOSITE: Caldo Tlalpeno.

CALDO DE ALBONDIGAS

(Albondigas Soup)

*Traditionally, there are plenty of meatballs in this soup –
the recipe calls for generous portions of meat.*

◆

S E R V E S 4

**Albondigas (see Albondiguitas page 38/39)
8 cups/2 1/3 pt beef stock
1 small onion, chopped
2 tomatoes, chopped
1 medium potato, diced
1 medium carrot, cut in rings
1 courgette (zucchini), cut in rings
Large pinch oregano
Salt and pepper to taste**

◆ Combine all the ingredients except the meatballs, which
should be about the size of a golf-ball or a little smaller.
Bring to the boil. Carefully insert the meatballs with a
spoon, one by one. Simmer for at least an hour.

OPPOSITE: Woman in Inchitan.
ABOVE: Caldo de Albondigas.

SOPA DE FIDEOS

(Vermicelli Soup)

*If you make it thin, this is a soup. If you decrease the
amount of stock, increase the quantities of the other
ingredients, and add some minced (ground) meat, you have
a dish which is more akin to spaghetti bolognaise. Both
versions are, of course, authentic. This is for the thinner
version:*

◆

S E R V E S 6

**100 g/4 oz vermicelli, broken up
1 tbsp lard
1 or 2 cloves garlic, finely chopped
6 cups/1·5 1/2½ pt beef stock
Half a small onion, finely chopped
1 can tomatoes, chopped with their liquid
1 tsp dried oregano
Salt and pepper**

◆ Fry the vermicelli in the lard until it is golden – about
5 minutes. Stir constantly to avoid burning. Reduce the
heat; add the garlic and fry for another 30 seconds to 1
minute to soften the garlic and pre-cook it. Add the rest of
the ingredients and bring to the boil. Simmer for half an
hour, stirring occasionally.

DRY SOUPS

As already described, 'dry' soups are not really dry at all; they take their name from the fact that they use some sort of dry ingredient – rice, pasta or even stale tortillas – to absorb some of the stock. Some people make them as very conventional soups, with just a few of the 'dry' ingredients; others simmer them with plenty of the 'dry' ingredients until the broth has almost all evaporated or been absorbed.

◆

SERVES 4

CHILAQUILES

(Tortilla Soup)

1 large or 2 small tomatoes
12 corn tortillas
Lard or olive oil for frying
1 medium onion, chopped
2 cloves garlic
4 cups/1 l/1½ pt chicken stock
Salt and pepper

◆ Halve and grill (broil) the tomato or 'dry-fry' it.

◆ The tortillas should be slightly dry; stale ones are ideal. Cut them into strips abot 1·5×5 cm (½×2 in). Deep-fry them until they are crisp and brown. Set them aside; pour off all but a tablespoon of the lard or oil.

◆ Fry the onion and garlic until golden-brown. In a blender, purée them with the tomato. Return the mixture to the frying pan with another tablespoon of lard or oil. Fry until thick, stirring constantly.

◆ Add the broth. Simmer for half an hour. Season to taste. Pour over the crisp tortillas in individual bowls.

VARIATIONS

Add diced leftover chicken or meat, or cheese, and offer the following separately as garnishes:

Sour cream
Chopped raw onion
Chopped hard-boiled eggs
Lime wedges
Dried pasilla chillies

▶ To prepare the chillies, remove the seeds and veins; tear into pieces and deep-fry for a few seconds, until crumbly. You can do them at the same time as the tortillas.

SOPA DE ARROZ

(Rice Dry Soup)

This is a somewhat drier dry soup than Chilaquiles. The first time you make it, it may even be too dry; the second time, you may over-compensate and make it too soupy. By the third time, though, you should have the technique weighed off. For basic stock, you can use meat, chicken or even vegetable stock. Check the rice for stones, etc, before you cook it, but do not wash it – or, if you must wash it, let it dry thoroughly (spread out in the oven at the lowest setting) before you use it.

◆

SERVES 4

1 cup/225 g/8 oz dry rice
2 tbsp olive or peanut oil
1 small onion, chopped
2–4 cloves garlic, finely chopped or mashed
4 cups/1 l/1½ pt stock
Salt and pepper

◆ Fry the rice in the oil, stirring frequently, until it is lightly golden – this should take about 10 minutres. Halfway through this cooking time, add the onion and garlic. Add the stock; season to taste; and cook, covered, at a very low heat for half an hour. Adjust the quantities of soup stock next time if the texture is not quite to your liking. You may also care to substitute tomato juice for up to one-third of the volume of stock.

VARIATIONS

▶ You can add all kinds of things with the onions, halfway through cooking the rice, to create richer soups. Quantities are not critical: add whatever you have, like, or can afford:

Mushrooms
Cooked chicken or meat
Serrano or jalapeno peppers
Chorizo or other sausage
Peas

▶ If you want to add seafood – shrimps, chunks of lobster, or crab – then do so at the same time that you add the stock; these ingredients are not fried beforehand, as it would only make them tough.

OPPOSITE: Chilaquiles.

BUDIN DE TORTILLAS

This is rather like a drier version of the Chilaquiles on page 48; it is also known as budin azteca.

◆

SERVES 4

3 large poblano or Anaheim chillies
12 corn tortillas
Fat for frying
250 g/½ lb cooked chicken, meat or fish (optional)
175 g/6 oz grated (shredded) Jack or
Cheddar cheese
1¼ cups/300 ml/½ pt sour cream
2 cups/450 ml/16 fl oz Mole Verde (page 25)
Salt and pepper
Thinly sliced onion and sliced radish for garnish

◆ Roast, peel and de-seed/de-vein the chillies as for Chiles Rellenos (page 36). Cut into strips.
◆ Soften the tortillas by frying for a few seconds. Divide the chillies and the chicken meat or fish into three portions; divide the cheese, cream and mole into four portions.
◆ The bottom layer, in a 23 cm (9 in) square pan, is three tortillas. Next follows meat, chilli, cheese, cream and mole. Next come three more tortillas, and the same mixture

again; and then repeat once more. The top shell or crust is tortillas and cheese/cream/mole, but not meat or chillies – they would only go dry.
◆ Bake at 175°C/350°F/Gas 4 for about 30 minutes. Garnish with onion and radish, and serve.

MACARONI AND HAM

This popular recipe is a true 'pasta' dish, and certainly one that is quite dry.

◆

SERVES 4

450 g/1 lb macaroni elbows
⅔ cup/125 g/4 oz cooked peas
½ cup/125 ml/4 fl oz sour cream (Mexican if
possible)
125 g/4 oz cooked ham, diced
2 heaped tbsp chopped coriander leaves
Salt and pepper
Tomatoes for garnish (optional)

◆ Boil the macaroni. Drain it thoroughly, and let it cool (or serve it warm). Add all the other ingredients, and mix well. Garnish with sliced tomatoes, if you like.

LEFT: Macaroni and Ham;
OPPOSITE: Preparing food in Ameyatapec, Guerrero.

51

FISH

Mexico's coasts teem with an extraordinary variety of fish. Most are cooked very simply: one favourite approach is to grill (broil) them over a slow fire, so that they are half-smoked by the time they are cooked. Fillets of larger fish are grilled (broiled) or fried, and served with various appetizing sauces. Here are some of the less obvious and more unusual ways to prepare fish.

◆

CEVICHE

Ceviche or seviche is fish pickled in lime juice. As usual, there are many ways of making it: some let the fish marinade in the lime juice before adding the other ingredients, some marinade the lot together, and the marinading times vary from half an hour to eight hours or more, depending on whom you believe. Some add olive oil, and even bell peppers; oregano adds another dimension; and some people heretically omit the serrano chillies. Note that Mexicans habitually call limes 'limones'; lemon juice will do, but lime juice is better.
The traditional fish is mackerel, though other fatty fishes also have history on their side. Mackerel is, however, messy and time-consuming to prepare, as well as tasting too strongly fishy for some people. It also makes for a coarse, mushy ceviche rather than an attactive-looking one. You can do just as well with fillets of any fish you like: fresh yellowtail and tuna are both delicious prepared this way, and sole, sea bass and red snapper are common choices.

◆

SERVES 6

1 kg/2 lb very fresh fish (see above)
2 large onions
3 medium-size, fully ripe tomatoes
5 limes
5 serrano chillies
Coriander
Salt and pepper

◆ Cut the fish into approx. 10–15 mm (½ in) cubes. Slice the onions into rings; chop the tomatoes, chillies and cilantro (coriander) as finely as possible. Squeeze the limes. Mix together, season and leave for at least half an hour at room temperature, turning frequently to ensure that the fish is evenly treated by the lime juice, which 'cooks' or pickles it. Refrigerate until served; it will keep overnight with no problem, though 24 hours is probably the limit.

Pour off any surplus lime-juice before serving. Serve cold on tortillas or tostadas (page 16); on biscuits; or in tacos, garnished with salad.

'DRUNKEN SQUID'

(Polpos Borrachos)

The outer envelope of the squid is what you cook. You can buy prepared squid; alternatively, preparing a whole squid is easier (and less unpleasant) than it looks. Salt your hands to get a good grip; grip the tentacles in one hand and the body in the other, and pull them apart. The tentacles will pull away, complete with the entrails. Feed the tentacles to the cat.

◆

SERVES 6

1 kg/2 lb squid
⅔ cup/150 ml/4 fl oz brandy
6 cups/1.5 l/48 oz Basic Tomato Sauce (page 25)
1¼ cups/300 ml/8 fl oz red wine
Salt and pepper
Olives and capers for garnish

◆ Clean the squid with plenty of salt. Pound it thoroughly with a rolling-pin or old-fashioned wooden potato-masher. Marinade for an hour (or more) in the brandy.
◆ Add just enough water to cover the squid; bring to the boil; simmer gently until tender. Drain, reserving the broth; cut the squid into approx. 2–3 cm (½–1 in) squares.
◆ Mix the broth, the tomato sauce, and the wine. Add pepper and salt. Simmer the squid in this for another half-hour. Serve with boiled rice; garnish with olives and capers. A robust Californian wine is ideal both for cooking and for accompanying this dish.

OPPOSITE: Preparing fish in Inchitan.

CALDO DE PESCADO

(Fish Stew)

The cheapest version of this (and in many eyes, the most delicate and delicious) is made with fish-heads. For the more dainty-minded gourmet, buy fillets of fish.

◆

S E R V E S 4

1 small onion, chopped finely
1 tbsp olive oil
2 medium red tomatoes
900 g/2 lb white fish in bite-size pieces
Small handful coriander leaves, chopped
3 cloves garlic, finely chopped
2 bay leaves
1 tsp dried oregano
Juice of 2 lemons or limes
4 cups/1 l/32 fl oz water
Salt and pepper

◆ Soften the onion in the oil. Add the chopped tomatoes and cook for a little longer – a minute or two. Add the remaining ingredients. Bring to the boil; reduce the heat; simmer for an hour or so.

PESCADO IN ESCABECHE

Strictly, escabeche or escaveche is a vinegar sauce which is used to pickle cooked meat, chicken or fish; it is also served in its own right as a sauce or relish. The recipe was presumably intended, originally, as a way of preserving fish: pescado in escabeche will keep for several weeks.

◆

S E R V E S 6

6 large fish fillets
Olive oil for frying
Escabeche sauce (page 27)

◆ Any firm fish is appropriate; huachinango or red snapper is excellent; sole or sea bass is good, too, but cheap, frozen fish can be greatly improved with this technique. Fry the fish fillets in a little oil until they are thoroughly cooked – three or four minutes on each side, starting with fish at room temperature (not chilled, and certainly not frozen). Marinate the fish in a glass dish in the refrigerator, turning occasionally, for up to three days: at the very least, leave it overnight.

ABOVE: Escabeche; OPPOSITE: Church scene in Yucatan.

HUACHINANGO YUCATECO

(Red Snapper, Yucatan-style)

If you are unable to find the authentic red snapper, try this dish with sole or sea bass instead. Try also pargo or sea bream.

◆

S E R V E S 4

2 small bell peppers, one red, one green
1 medium onion, chopped
2 cloves garlic
4 tbsp/60 g/2 oz butter
2 tbsp chopped coriander leaves
1 tsp whole cumin
½ tsp grated orange rind
½ cup/125 ml/4 fl oz fresh-squeezed orange juice
1 red snapper, 2 kg/4–5 lb, cleaned and scaled
6–8 sliced black olives
Salt and pepper to taste
1 large or 2 small avocados, for garnish

◆ Seed, de-vein and chop the peppers. Chop the onion. Chop the garlic, finely. Fry them all together in 2 table-spoons butter, until softened. Add the coriander, cumin, orange rind and orange juice; season to taste. Simmer for two minutes.

◆ Thickly grease the bottom of a large, shallow casserole with the rest of the butter. Put the fish in the casserole and cover it with the sauce. Scatter the olives over the top.

◆ Bake for about 30 minutes, basting occasionally with the sauce. Serve hot, garnished with thin slices of avocado.

POMPANO EN PAPILOTTE

If you can't find pompano, any fairly firm, modestly sized white fish will do.

◆

S E R V E S 4

1 kg/2 lb pompano fillets
½ cup/125 g/4 oz cooked shrimp
½ cup/125 g/4 oz cooked crabmeat
4 parchment bags, or pieces of buttered foil
2 tsp butter
2 tsp flour
⅔ cup/110 ml/¼ pt chicken stock
Salt and pepper

◆ Divide the fish fillets, shrimps and crabmeat equally between the four bags. (An alternative is to make 'parcels' out of lightly buttered foil.)

◆ Make a *roux* of the butter and flour by melting the butter and stirring in the flour. Add the stock gradually, stirring constantly, to make a thick, smooth sauce. Divide between the four bags. Fold the bags closed, and place them in a casserole. Bake at 160°C/325°F/Gas 3 for about 35–40 minutes; the bags should be puffed and brown. Serve hot, in the bags.

O P P O S I T E : Carnival in
Guadalupe; R I G H T :
Huachinango Yucatana.

MEAT AND POULTRY

Mexican meat and poultry is usually full of flavour, but not as tender as the meat you buy in North America or Northern Europe. Long, slow cooking tenderizes it, and retains the full flavour.
To a very large extent, all similar-looking cuts of meat (and even some very dissimilar ones) are interchangeable in Mexican cooking. Beef is widely used; so is pork; chicken is highly regarded; much more lamb is eaten than north of the border, and goat (especially young goat or kid) is prepared the same way. There are also delicacies which are extremely difficult, if not impossible, to obtain outside Mexico, such as armadillo and iguana.
In stews, or under a 'mole', various kinds of different meats are often mixed: pork and chicken is a common combination.

◆

CARNE ASADA

In Spain, 'asada' means 'roast'. In Mexico, it's a way of cooking a steak, preferably marinated. The better the steak you use, the better the results will be, but because the citrus fruits tenderize the meat you can get surprisingly good quality from quite modest cuts – there is no need to go to fillet steak (filet mignon) for this dish. Also, strong-flavoured dark beers such as Modelo Negra or even Guinness are ideal as ingredients or accompaniments.
Serve with Mexican rice, refried beans and salad.

◆

SERVES 4

1 medium or small onion
1 large lime
1 small orange
⅓ cup/75 ml/2½ fl oz beer
1 cup/225 ml/8 fl oz soy sauce
1 kg/2¼ lb steak
1 bunch spring (green) onions
Salt and pepper to taste

◆ Squeeze the lime and the orange; mix with the beer and the soy sauce. Add the onion, sliced in rings. Marinate the meat for at least an hour, turning frequently to ensure that it is evenly coated. Cook on a spit; or on a barbecue. Grill the cebollitas (onions) as a garnish.

BISTECK RANCHERO

This is a traditional way to cook (rather tough) steak for the merienda or 'second breakfast'. As is often the case in Mexican cooking, the steak is far from rare: rather, it is cooked once by frying and a second time by steam in the covered pan. Thick steak would be intolerable this way; thin steak has an excellent flavour.

◆

SERVES 2

350 g/¾ lb steak, sliced thin
2 tsp olive oil
Salt and pepper to taste
½ onion, sliced thickly
1 large tomato
1 green California chilli, sliced into 'wheels'
2 chopped serrano chillies
2 tbsp chicken broth

◆ Fry the meat in the oil with the salt and pepper. When it is almost done, add the other ingredients and stir to coat the meat thoroughly. Cover, and cook well.
◆ Serve with refried beans.

OPPOSITE: Bisteck Ranchero; BELOW: Carne Asada.

ABOVE: Carne Molida Cruda; OPPOSITE: The Church of San Juan Chamula in Chiapas.

CARNE MOLIDA CRUDA

Carne molida cruda – literally, 'meat ground raw' – is a Mexican version of steak tartare. The lime juice tenderizes the meat, but adds quite a strong flavour.

◆

S E R V E S   4

2 jalapeno chillies, finely chopped
Half a small onion
450 g/1 lb fillet steak
(other good, lean cuts will do)
Salt and pepper to taste

◆ In a food processor, chop first the chillies, then the onion. Remove. Cut the steak into cubes; remove fat and membranes; chop in the food processor. Do not chop too finely: there should still be a meaty texture, rather than beef toothpaste. Mix all the ingredients together, using plenty of fresh-ground black pepper (1 teaspoon is not too much), but little salt: raw meat is fairly salty.

◆ The longer you leave the meat, the more pronounced the lime flavour will be, and the less obvious the meat flavour. After an hour or so, the lime hides the meat flavour. For carnivores, therefore, serve immediately: for others, leave for an hour. Devotees of steak tartare may prefer the French dish; but the Mexican version is worth trying.

ESTOFADO DE LENGUA

(Stewed tongue)

Stewed tongue, like raw meat, is one of those dishes which may not sound immediately appetizing. If you can bring yourself to prepare it, though, it is unquestionably delicious.

◆

S E R V E S   8 – 1 0

Fresh beef tongue – 2–2·5 kg/about 5 lb
1 small onion, peeled
5 cloves garlic
8 black peppercorns
Salt to taste (1 to 2 tbsp)

◆ Ask your butcher to trim the tongue for boiling. Put the whole tongue in a large saucepan with enough water to cover, with the other ingredients. Bring to the boil; simmer gently until tender (about three to four hours). Remove from the heat; as soon as the tongue is cool enough to handle, take it out of the broth; skin it (discarding the skin); and return it to the stock.

T H E   S A U C E

1 small tortilla
2 anchos chillies
2 tbsp lard
60 g/2 oz whole, unpeeled almonds
1 kg/2 lb whole, fresh tomatoes finely chopped
2 tbsp sesame seeds
2 cm/½ in stick cinnamon
Large pinch (⅛ tsp) each thyme, marjoram, oregano
Green olives to garnish
Jalapenos in escabeche as a side-dish

◆ Leave the tortilla out to dry for a while – or preferably use a stale tortilla.

◆ Remove the seeds and veins from the chillies; fry them lightly in the lard. Drain; transfer to a blender. The same lard is also used to fry the almonds, until they are well browned; the tortilla until it is crisp; and the tomatoes (over a high heat for about 10 minutes, scraping and stirring constantly). Crush the almonds and tortillas before you add them to the blender, then add the tomatoes.

◆ Toast the sesame seeds in a dry frying pan, or on a griddle, until they are golden. Shake constantly to avoid popping. Transfer to a pestle and mortar or spice grinder; grind to crack and break the hulls. They smell delicious when you do this. Then add them to the blender with the cnnamon and herbs, and blend to get a very smooth sauce.

◆ Fry this sauce in the lard; reduce the heat, stirring frequently, and cook for about 10 minutes until it just coats the spoon with which you are stirring it. If it is too thick, add some of the stock from the tongue.

◆ Slice the tongue thinly; arrange on a serving-plate; and mask with some of the sauce. Serve the rest of the sauce separately. Garnish with green olives. Serve with plain boiled rice; hand jalapenos in escabeche for those who like their food a little spicier.

CARNE CON CHILE COLORADO

This is utterly different from the Tex-Mex version that most people know: rather than being a mixture of cheap minced (ground) beef, beans and tomato sauce, it consists of large chunks of tender meat in a thick, smooth, rich sauce. Making the sauce is quite a lot of work, but the result is worth it. You can make it with either beef or pork.

◆

S E R V E S   4

8 middle-sized dried chillies: California or New Mexico type
$\frac{1}{2}$ tsp cumin seeds
3 cloves garlic, peeled
1 small onion, chopped
1 tsp dried oregano
700 g/1 $\frac{1}{2}$ lb lean, boneless meat
Oil or lard for frying
2 cups/450 ml/16 fl oz water or stock
Salt to taste

◆ Prepare the dried chillies as described on page 15. While they are soaking, grind the cumin seeds in a pestle and mortar or spice grinder.

◆ Drain the chillies, but keep one cup of the soaking liquid. Add the garlic, onion, oregano and fresh-ground cumin. Purée the lot, with the soaking liquid, in a blender. Blend until smooth, then strain through a wire sieve: this is one of the most time-consuming parts, but it makes for a wonderfully smooth sauce.

◆ Cut the meat into approx. 2.5 cm (1 in) cubes, and fry in a heavy, deep skillet with a little lard or oil until browned all over – about 10 minutes. Keep turning the meat and scraping the pan.

◆ Add the strained sauce; continue to cook, stirring and scraping frequently to avoid burning, for a few minutes (5 at most). The purée should be thick and rather darker than when you started. Add the water or stock; bring to a boil, and simmer over a low heat for at least an hour, stirring occasionally. If the sauce gets too thick, add a little more water or stock. It is ready when the meat is *very* tender.

TEX-MEX CHILI CON CARNE

While this is hardly a traditional Mexican dish, it is cheap and tastes good. It is also easy to make, and goes down very well at parties when accompanied by plenty of crusty French bread. Adjust the garlic and the chilli seasoning to taste: a tablespoon of pasilla will be very mild, while other types will be hotter. For extra heat, add up to $\frac{1}{2}$ teaspoon chopped, dried chillies.

◆

S E R V E S   4 – 6

2 medium onions, chopped
2–6 cloves garlic, crushed
4 tbsp olive oil or lard
750 g/1 $\frac{1}{2}$ lb minced (ground) beef
1 heaped tbsp chilli powder
1 standard can tomatoes
1 tbsp cumin seed
1 bay leaf
1 cup/250 ml/8 fl oz beef stock
3 tbsp tomato purée (paste)
1 standard can red kidney beans
Salt

◆ Fry the onions and garlic in the oil or lard until the onions are soft and translucent. Add the beef, and fry for 5–10 minutes until it is brown and crumbly. Add the chilli powder, and fry for another 20 seconds or so, until the powder is well mixed with the beef, then add the tomatoes (undrained) and the other ingredients except the beans. Bring to the boil. Simmer, covered, for an hour (more will not hurt). About 15 minutes before serving, stir in the beans, and simmer some more.

◆ Serve with white rice or (as already mentioned) with crusty bread. For a traditional Texan touch, have plenty of beer on hand.

OPPOSITE: Carne Con Chile Colorado; RIGHT: Scene in Tepoztlan.

ROPA VIEJA

(Shredded Beef Stew)

Literally 'old clothes', ropa vieja is in fact a thick, meaty stew of shredded beef. The trick lies in cooking the meat until it is almost falling apart, then teasing it into shreds with two forks. Prepare the meat first.

◆

S E R V E S   4 — 6

1 kg/2 lb chuck steak, cubed
1 large onion, sliced
2 cloves garlic, finely chopped
2 tbsp vinegar
2 cups/450 ml/16 fl oz water or stock
1 can or 500 g/1 lb fresh tomatoes

◆ In a flame proof casserole or Dutch oven, bring the meat to a boil with all the other ingredients except the tomatoes.

◆ Cover, and simmer over a very low heat for two or three hours. After the first hour or two, add the tomatoes: they should simmer with the meat for at least 45 minutes. When the meat is *very* tender, fish it out with a fork, and shred it on to a plate. When all the meat is shredded, return it to the stock. Meanwhile, prepare the following:

2 bell peppers, one red and one green
2 boiled potatoes
2 tbsp olive oil

◆ De-seed, de-vein and slice the peppers. Slice the potatoes. Fry them both together in the oil in a skillet or frying pay until the peppers are tender, then add to the meat. Cook very gently until the liquid has almost all evaporated.

◆ Serve with boiled rice or tortillas – or boiled potatoes if you're not too much of a traditionalist.

OPPOSITE: Ropa Veija.

BIRRIA

Preparing authentic birria is next to impossible: traditionally, a whole lamb or kid was seasoned with an adobo sauce, then cooked in a barbecue-pit lined with maguey leaves. The leaves kept the animal from overheating, and the result was meat that was slowly steam- and smoke-cooked for many hours, until it was so tender that it was falling apart. Tacos de Birria are widely advertised on roadside food-stands in Mexico. In practice, you can make a good home-cooked birria in several ways. The first is the more traditional method.

◆

TRADITIONAL BIRRIA

S E R V E S   4 — 8

About 3 kg/6–7 lb meat (see below)
Adobo Sauce (see page 26)
1 kg/2 lb tomatoes
Salt and pepper
Oregano and chopped onion to garnish

◆ The traditional meat is lamb, but you can equally well use pork or goat (or kid), and some people like to use mixed meats or to add a chicken. Cheaper cuts, such as breast of lamb, etc, are traditional. Leave the meat in big chunks; slash deeply; rub in salt, and coat thickly with adobo sauce. Leave to season overnight – say 16–18 hours.

◆ Put a roasting grid or rack inside a large flameproof casserole or Dutch oven; add enough water to lap at the bottom of the rack, but no higher. Place the meat on the rack; cover, and seal the cover with a flour-and-water paste. Cook for three or four hours at 175°C/350°F/Gas 4 or use a pressure-cooker and follow the manufacturers' instructions. Alternatively, put the rack and meat inside a large roasting bag, with no additional stock, and cook at 150°C/300°F/Gas 2 for at least 3 hours.

◆ Once the meat is cooked, strain off the stock at the bottom; cool, and remove the fat. If necessary, add water or stock to make 2 cups/450 ml/16 fl oz.

◆ Bake, grill (broil) or 'dry-fry' the halved tomatoes – in other words, cook them without fat. Blend (in a blender) to a smooth sauce. Add the sauce to the stock and bring to a boil in a saucepan.

◆ Serve the meat, cut into slices or chunks, in individual bowls with ½ cup/110 ml/4 fl oz sauce. Sprinkle with chopped onion and oregano; serve with hot tortillas. This recipe serves 4–8, depending on the amount of bone in the original meat, and the size of your guests' appetites!

'BIRRIA' STEW

Another approach, which is more like a stew and less like a traditional birria, is made as follows:

◆

SERVES 4 – 8

4 anchos chillies
About 3 kg/6–7 lb meat (as for previous recipe)
5–10 cloves garlic
7 cloves
1 stick cinnamon
1 tbsp dried oregano
2 cans tomatoes, undrained

$\frac{1}{2}$ cup/110 ml/4 fl oz wine vinegar
Salt and pepper
1 bottle beer
1 large red onion to garnish

◆ Prepare the chillies as described on page 15. Cut the meat into serving-size pieces.

◆ Blend together the drained, soaked chillies with the garlic, cloves, cinnamon, oregano, tomato, vinegar and seasoning. You may need to do this in batches. When the sauce is smooth, add the beer. Blend again.

◆ Put the meat in a flameproof casserole or Dutch oven; pour over the sauce; cover; and simmer until very tender, at least 3 hours.

◆ Serve with thinly sliced onion and hot tortillas.

CARNE DE RES CON NOPALITOS

Nopalitos are the fresh, young sprouts of some types of cactus – with the spines removed, needless to say! Bottled or canned nopalitos, available in most Mexican stores, are fine for this dish.

◆

S E R V E S 4 – 6

1·3 kg/3 lb beef, cut in 5 cm/2 in cubes
4 tbsp olive oil or lard
1 large onion, finely chopped
2–4 cloves garlic, finely chopped
1 can or bottle nopalitos
1 300 g/10 oz can tomatillos
6 canned or 3 fresh serrano chillies, chopped
4 tbsp tomato purée (paste)
1 cup/225 ml/8 fl oz beef stock
One handful fresh coriander, chopped
Salt and pepper

◆ Fry the beef in the lard or olive oil, a few cubes at a time, until well browned. Transfer to a flameproof casserole or Dutch oven. In the same fat, fry the onion and garlic until golden. Add to the beef.
◆ Drain the nopalitos, and rinse them thoroughly. Add to the beef, onions and garlic with the other ingredients (don't drain the tomatillos). Bring to the boil, and simmer gently until the beef is very tender – 2½ to 3 hours.

CARNE DE RES CON TOMATILLOS

It is surprising how different this is from the very similar-sounding Carne de Res con Nopalitos.

◆

S E R V E S 6

Generous 1 kg/2½ lb round steak
2 tbsp lard or olive oil
1 onion, sliced
2 cloves garlic, finely chopped
300–400 g/8–12 oz chorizo
2 or more canned serrano chillies
OR 1 or more fresh serrano chillies, sliced
1 handful fresh coriander, chopped
1 300 g/10 oz tomatillos
Salt and pepper
12 new potatoes

◆ In a heavy frying pan or skillet, brown the meat on both sides. Transfer to a flameproof casserole or Dutch oven.
◆ In the same oil or lard, fry the onion and garlic until translucent. Add the skinned, diced chorizo; fry some more, until some of the fat has rendered out of the sausage. Drain off excess fat; add the onion-garlic-chorizo mixture to the beef. Add the other ingredients, *except* the potatoes. Simmer for at least 2 hours: the beef should be very tender.
◆ Meanwhile, boil the potatoes. When the beef is tender, add the potatoes; cook for another few minutes (5–10 minutes until the potatoes are hot through.

RIGHT: Carne de Res con Nopalitos; LEFT: Pots for sale in Chicapa Guerrero.

MEAT AND POULTRY

67

PICADILLO

Picadillo can be made with chopped, minced (ground) or finely sliced beef. This version is made with thin-sliced beef cut into strips about 1 cm ($\frac{1}{4}$–$\frac{1}{2}$ in) wide and 5 cm (2 in) long. Also, the most authentic recipes call for chayote, a sort of firm-fleshed gourd sometimes known as the 'vegetable pear'. The next best alternative is a large, firm tart cooking-apple, though the flavour will not be quite as good. If you cannot get chayote, just leave it out.

◆

SERVES 4–6 AS A MAIN DISH

1 kg/2 lb lean beef
4 tbsp olive oil or lard
1 medium onion
2–4 cloves garlic
1 chayote, peeled and cubed
1 large potato, peeled and cubed
2 large tomatoes, cut in chunks
2 carrots, peeled and sliced
1 courgette (zucchini), sliced
30 g/1 oz raisins
3 or more canned sliced jalapeno chillies
10 pimiento-stuffed olives, halved
Large pinch each of cinnamon and cloves
(about $\frac{1}{8}$ tsp)
Salt and pepper
1 cup/200 g/6 oz peas
60 g/2 oz slivered almonds to garnish

◆ Cut the beef in strips, as described above; or chop finely. Fry in a heavy skillet until brown; add the onions and garlic. When these are golden, add all the other ingredients except the almonds and peas. Bring to the boil; simmer for 20–30 minutes, according to how well done you like the vegetables. Five minutes (or less) before serving, add the peas and stir them in.

◆ Fry the slivered almonds in a little olive oil (or almond oil), shaking the pan constantly to avoid burning. When they are golden-brown, sprinkle them over the picadillo.

68

PICADILLO DE LA COSTA

To see how different picadillo from different areas can be, try making this coastal version.

◆

S E R V E S   4 — 6

450 g/1 lb minced (ground) pork
450 g/1 lb minced (ground) veal
2 tbsp olive oil
2 onions, finely chopped
2 cloves garlic, finely chopped
2 large tomatoes, peeled, seeded and chopped
2—4 fresh serrano chillies
3 thick slices fresh pineapple
3 plantanos or bananas
3 pears or apples, peeled and cored
Large pinch each of ground cinnamon and cloves
(about $\frac{1}{8}$ tsp)

Salt and pepper
60 g/2 oz slivered almonds to garnish

◆ Brown the meat in the oil, using a heavy frying pan or skillet; drain off excess fat. Add the onions and garlic, and cook until golden. Add the tomatoes, and the finely sliced chillies; simmer for a quarter of an hour. Season to taste.

◆ Peel the pineapple slices and cut them in chunks. Cut the plantanos into slices 1·2 cm (½ in) thick: if you cannot get plantanos, use slightly underripe bananas. Cut the pears or apples into chunks. Add the fruit and spices to the picadillo; cook for about 15 minutes more. (Cooking the fruit for too long will cause it to disintegrate.)

◆ Fry the almonds as in the previous recipe, and garnish the picadillo with them.

OPPOSITE: Picadillo; BELOW: Scene in Inchitan.

POZOLE

(Pork and Hominy)

Pozole is a classic, simple peasant dish. Basically, it consists of a cheap, bony cut of pork – head, feet or back ribs – boiled with garlic until it is soft, then cooked with hominy and chilli. This recipe calls for ribs; if you want to be very traditional, use half a pig's head instead. Everyone should get a share of the ear, and the eye is allegedly reserved for an honoured guest. If you are feeling less traditional, substitute a pound of cubed lean pork for half the ribs. If you want rich man's pozole, use a chicken as well.

◆

S E R V E S 4

1 kg/2 lb pork ribs
1 small head garlic
1 medium onion (optional)
2 330 g/12 oz cans hominy
1 dried red ancho chilli
Salt
Garnish: onion, lettuce or cabbage, radish, tostadas and slices of lime

◆ Boil the pork ribs until they are soft, together with the garlic; add an onion if you like. Use just enough water to cover. When the meat begins to soften and shred, add it with its broth to the hominy and the torn-up chilli. Cook for one more hour.
◆ Serve with finely chopped onion, sliced lettuce or cabbage, radish, tostadas and slices of lime: these are added to the soup by each diner, according to preference.

MOLE DE OLLA

Moles de olla are stews made with chillies and various kinds of meat. As a change from those made with various types of meat, this Mole de Olla Estilo Atlixco (in the style of Atlixco) is made with two kinds of sausage, the spicy chorizo and the milder longanzina. You can of course vary the proportions of the two to suit your personal preferences.

◆

S E R V E S 6

6 ancho chillies
2 tbsp lard or olive oil
350 g/12 oz chorizo
350 g/12 oz longanzina
225 g/8 oz boneless stewing pork
1 1·5 kg/3½–4 lb chicken
2 tbsp sesame seeds
2 tbsp shelled, unsalted pumpkin seeds
60 g/2 oz almonds
1 medium onion
2–5 cloves garlic
1 large tomato
1 tsp oregano
2 cups/450 ml/16 fl oz chicken stock
Salt and pepper

◆ Prepare the chillies (see page 15). While they are soaking, skin and chop the chorizo and longanzina, and cut the chicken into serving-size pieces. Cube the pork.
◆ In the lard or oil, fry first the sausage, then the pork, then the chicken. Transfer to a flameproof casserole or Dutch oven.
◆ Toast the sesame seeds in a dry frying pan or skillet, shaking frequently to avoid popping. Grind in a spice-grinder or pestle and mortar. If you omit the step, and simply throw the seeds into the blender (below), you will miss at least half the flavour.
◆ In a blender, combine the sesame seeds, pumpkin seeds, almonds, chillies, onion, garlic, tomato and oregano. Blend until smooth. Fry this mixture in the fat remaining from the sausage, etc for about 5 minutes, stirring and scraping constantly: the sauce should darken and thicken appreciably. Add the stock; mix well, and pour over the meats. Bring to the boil, reduce the heat, and simmer gently for an hour or more – as usual, the longer you cook this dish (within reason), the better it tastes.

LEFT: Cheese and sausages in Toluca; OPPOSITE: Preparing papaya in Mexico City.

70

OPPOSITE: Puerco con Repollo y Elote; RIGHT: The City of the Dead.

CALABACITAS CON CARNE DE PUERCO

(Pork with Courgettes [Zucchini])

This is a straightforward dish. In the original version, the ribs were chopped into small pieces; using the meatier country-style ribs gives a similar flavour, but fewer awkward bits of bone. Soy sauce may not seem to be very Mexican, but it appears in an increasing number of Mexican dishes.

◆

S E R V E S 4

1 kg/2 lb country-style pork ribs (4 ribs)
6 courgettes (zucchini), sliced
1 medium onion, sliced
2 medium tomatoes, sliced
2 green California chillies
OR 1 red bell pepper
2 cups/450 ml/16 fl oz meat stock
1 tbsp soy sauce
Fat for frying
Salt and pepper

◆ Fry the ribs until they are golden, season to taste. Pour off excess fat. Add all the other ingredients, cover, and cook slowly for at least one hour – two hours is not too long. Serve accompanied by arroz cacero rojo – rice cooked with a little pasilla chilli powder to add colour and flavour. It also goes well with boiled or mashed potatoes, with sweet corn as a vegetable.

PUERCO CON REPOLLO Y ELOTE

(Pork with Cabbage and Corn)

A modern Mexican would probably make this with a can of corn. Frozen corn is good, too, but for the very best flavour you need to scrape the corn from 2 or 3 fresh ears.

◆

S E R V E S 6

750 g/1½ lb pork ribs, chopped
1 medium onion, cut in rings
2 large tomatoes, cut in rings
2 cloves garlic
Pinch of cumin seed
8 peppercorns
2 tbsp vinegar
1 medium cabbage, sliced
350 g/12 oz sweet corn
Salt and pepper

◆ Using a heavy flameproof casserole or Dutch oven, cook the pork in just enough water to cover. When the ribs are tender (at least an hour), add the onion and the tomato. Cook for a few minutes longer.
◆ In a blender, combine the garlic, the cumin, the peppercorns and the vinegar. Add to the meat, together with the cabbage and corn. Stir well and season: the meal is ready when the cabbage is cooked. Serve with boiled rice.

LEFT: Mancha Mantel;
OPPOSITE: Ameyatepec scene.

MANCHA MANTEL

('Tablecloth-stainer')

A 'mancha mantel' is a 'tablecloth-stainer'; and when you see the colour of this dish, you will see why. You may even want to change into old clothes to eat it. You can make it with pork, or chicken, or (as here) a mixture of both. Other variations include using firm, tart cooking apples (if you can't get jicama); tomatillos; pears; peas; and even canned pineapple instead of fresh (though the texture will be completely different).

◆

SERVES 4 – 6

350 g/¾ lb boneless stewing pork
1 chicken, about 1·5 kg/3½ lb
3 tbsp fat or oil
24 almonds
2–5 cm/1–2 in cinnamon bark
1½ tbsp sesame seeds
5 ancho chillies
2 medium tomatoes
6 cloves garlic (optional), unpeeled
1 thick slice pineapple, cubed
1 small plantano or 1 large slightly underripe banana
1 small (250 g/½ lb) jicama
Salt (try 1 tbsp)
1 cup/200 g/6 oz peas (optional)

◆ Cut the pork into 4 cm (1½ in) cubes. Put in a saucepan with just enough water to cover, and a little salt. Bring to the boil; simmer for 25 minutes. Drain; strain the stock and keep it. Add more water (or meat or chicken stock) to make 4 cups/scant 1 litre/32 fl oz.

◆ Cut the chicken into serving-sized pieces, and fry in the oil in a heavy flameproof casserole or Dutch oven; brown a few pieces at a time. In the same oil, fry the almonds with their skins; then the cinnamon bark; then the sesame seeds. Put the almonds, cinnamon and sesame seeds in a blender. De-seed and de-vein the chillies. In the little oil that is left, fry them too; add to the blender.

◆ Grill (broil) the halved tomatoes, or 'dry-fry' them in a frying pan with no added oil. When they are cooked, tip them into the blender.

◆ Cook the unpeeled garlic in a frying pan with no oil, or on a griddle. After 10–15 minutes, the cloves will be very soft and the blistered, blackened skins will be very easy to remove. Put the peeled garlic in the blender.

◆ Using just enough of the stock to free the blender blades (about 1¼ cups/250 ml/½ pt), purée all this. Use no more stock than you have to at this stage, or the sauce will be too thin.

◆ Re-heat what little oil is left in the casserole, and add the contents of the blender to it. Fry for 3–5 minutes, scraping and stirring constantly: the sauce should become dark and thick. Add the remainder of the stock, and bring to a simmer. Add the meat and fruit; salt to taste; then cook very gently for at least an hour, until the meat is tender and the vegetables are soft. If you are adding peas, put them in five minutes before serving: they will be hopelessly overcooked otherwise.

◆ Serve hot, with freshly made tortillas.

FAJITAS

A fajita is a cut of meat, not a way of cooking or presenting meat. Specifically, it is the 'skirt steak' or 'flank steak' from the area of the diaphragm, a rather tough piece of meat that is covered with a gristly membrane and thus requires both stripping and tenderizing. The 'outside skirt' is from the diaphragm itself, while the 'inside skirt' (la faja de adentro) is slightly tenderer and comes from the inner part of the flank. Traditionally, fajitas were a very cheap cut; they figure in a number of peasant dishes from many lands. In the more affluent areas of the United States, fajitas were often minced (ground) into cheap hamburger; the fajita as we understand it today is probably an early- to mid-twentieth-century Tex-Mex invention.

With most of the history out of the way, there is no question that well-prepared fajitas can be very good; and while other cuts of meat prepared in the same way will taste different, they are arguably even better than the real thing. Also, fajitas are insanely overpriced in many markets: in central California, when this book was being written, fajita prices were comparable with porterhouse and even fillet steaks (filet mignon). Fajitas and fajita-lookalikes can be eaten in the same way as steaks, or sliced, and put in a taco or burrito or even a pocket of pitta bread.

To prepare real fajitas, lay the meat on a cutting board and remove the fat – carefully – with a sharp knife. This is time-consuming. Next, remove the tough outer membrane. It helps if you have three arms: one to hold the steak, one to lift the membrane, and one to slide the knife along at the point of separation, helping the membrane peel off. Third, slit the meat with a very sharp knife, working both with and against the grain. Stab it repeatedly with a fork to tenderize it further. You can use a mallet, but it makes for a mushy piece of meat. So do proprietary tenderizers: the marinade should be all the tenderizer you need. The fajita is now ready to marinate.

If you are preparing other cuts fajita-style, you are spared all this. Marinate the meat in large slices, 1·2–2·5 cm (½–1 in) thick; after turning it several times to be sure it is evenly coated with marinade, leave it in the refrigerator for 12 to 24 hours. Slice the meat into strips 15 cm (6 in) long before you cook it.

◆ Take the meat out of the refrigerator an hour or two before you are going to cook it; having the meat at room temperature is one of the secrets of successful cooking, especially barbecuing. Cut the meat into strips 10–15 cm (4–6 in) long. Either fry the strips in a heavy iron frying pan or skillet with a minimum of oil, or grill (broil) them on a barbecue – the latter probably tastes better.

◆ Serve with warm 15 cm (6 in) flour tortillas and any or all of the following accompaniments: salsa; sliced onion; tomato; bell pepper; sour cream; guacamole or avocado; sliced lettuce; frijoles refritos; Mexican rice.

MARGARITA MARINADE

◆

3 parts lime juice
1 part Triple Sec
2 parts tequila

◆ The lime juice tenderizes it, the Triple Sec flavours and sweetens it, and the tequila flavours it. It works!

LIME MARINADE

◆

1 cup/225 ml/8 fl oz beef broth
Juice of 1 large lime
3 tbsp Worcestershire sauce
1 or 2 cloves garlic, finely chopped
1 tbsp chopped cilantro (coriander)

WINE MARINADE

½ cup/110 ml/4 fl oz really cheap, nasty red wine
(or use half-and-half red wine and red wine vinegar)
3 tbsp olive oil
1 or 2 cloves garlic, finely chopped
1 tbsp chopped coriander

OPPOSITE: Cooked Fajitas.

V A R I A T I O N S

▶ If you are just after unusual tastes, and are using (reasonably) tender meat to start with, mix and match from the following list of possible marinade ingredients:

Brandy or whisky (any variety) or rum
Red wine or sherry
Beer
Vinegar (wine, cider, etc)
Juice of any citrus fruit
Pineapple juice

Hot sauce, or dried red peppers soaked and pounded
Soy sauce or Worcestershire sauce
Onion, garlic
Fresh coriander, including freshly crushed seeds
Rosemary, basil, sage, thyme, oregano, cumin
Whole peppercorns, black or green

▶ If you have a sweet tooth, add sugar (brown or white) or honey. It doesn't really matter what you use: this is not a traditional peasant dish, though it is now sufficiently Mexicanized to be found in many restaurants in Mexico.

TAMALES

◆◆◆◆◆◆◆◆◆◆◆◆◆◆◆◆◆◆◆◆◆◆

Tamales are made from the same masa harina as corn tortillas (see page 16), though lard is added to the dough. Deceptively simple-looking, tamales are in fact surprisingly difficult to make: they fall apart, stick to the corn-husks in which they are steamed, and generally misbehave.

◆

M A K E S 1 6 — 2 4

◆ Use a basic masa, or for extra luxury make it with chicken, pork or beef stock. Mix 500 g/1 lb of this masa with about half as much lard. Cream the lard; it must be light and fluffy. Beat the dough and the lard together until you have a light, soft, slightly mushy dough. A spoonful of the dough should float in water.

◆ If you are using dried corn-husks, soak them in hot water to soften them; this takes about half an hour to an hour. Shake the water from the corn-husks. Put one tablespoon of dough in the centre of each husk; spread it out until it is about 1·2 cm (½ in) thick. Use your fingers or (much easier) a tortilla press. Put a tablespoon of filling in the centre of the dough; roll up the dough-plus-husk to enclose the filling, and fold the top and bottom of each husk over. Wrap another husk around the first, and tie the ends with string.

◆ Put the tamales in a steamer with the bottom end of the corn-husk down. Steam for about an hour, or until the dough starts to come away from the husks.

FILLING

**4–6 cloves garlic
3 California chillies
450 g/1 lb well-cooked beef, pork or chicken
1 ancho chilli**

◆ Prepare the chillies as described on page 15. While they are soaking, shred the meat with two forks.
◆ Liquidize the chillies in a blender with the garlic and a little of the soaking broth. Fry the purée for 5 minutes, stirring and scraping constantly, then add the shredded meat.

◆

VARIATIONS

▶ Variations in the masa include adding 1 cup/100 g/4 fl oz of cream to the stock used to make it, and adding ¼ teaspoon each of cumin and oregano plus one puréed, soaked dried chilli to the basic dough recipe.
▶ Variations in the filling include using tomatoes, onions, and herbs such as rosemary, thyme, oregano and cumin.

TAMALE PIE

A good way to get most of the flavour of tamales, without going to all the trouble with the corn-husks, is to make a tamale pie. Using the same masa as for the tamales in the previous recipe, line a greased 2 litre/2 qt casserole with the dough, reserving enough to cover the top.

CHICKEN TAMALE PIE

SERVES 6 – 8

**1 chicken, about 1·5 kg/3½–4 lb
6 dried red chillies (arbol, ancho)
1 large onion, chopped
5–10 cloves garlic, chopped
3 large tomatoes, peeled, de-seeded and chopped
OR 1 330 g/12 oz can peeled tomatoes
60 g/2 oz blanched almonds
100 g/4 oz raisins
2 tbsp lard or olive oil
Salt and pepper to taste**

◆ Boil the chicken in just enough water to cover, until very tender. When cool, strip the flesh from the bones. Save the broth; you can mix the masa using this. Throw away the fat, bones, and skin. Cut the meat into fairly large pieces.
◆ Remove the seeds from the chillies, and soak them in about a cup of water for an hour. Save the soaking water!
◆In a food processor, chop the onions, garlic, tomatoes, almonds, raisins and soaked chillies and enough of the soaking water to make a coarse purée. Cook this in the oil, stirring constantly, over a moderate heat for 5 minutes. Check seasoning.
◆ Put the chicken in the masa-lined casserole (see above) and pour *half* the sauce over it. Cover with the remaining masa. Bake at 180°C/350°F/Gas 4 for one hour. Heat the other half of the sauce to serve over the tamale pie.

PORK TAMALE PIE

◆ To make a pork tamale pie, use 1 kg/2¼ lb of pork, cut in 5 cm (2 in) cubes. Boil until tender (about 1½ hours). Make the masa with pork broth instead of chicken broth. Prepare as above, except that the sauce is:

**1 medium onion, chopped
3–6 cloves garlic, chopped
3 dried chillies
3 large tomatoes OR 1 can, as before
½ tsp ground coriander seed
1 tsp dried oregano (½ tsp fresh)
1 bay leaf**

OPPOSITE: Tamales; LEFT: Tamales in Inchitan.

CHICKEN

Chicken and turkey are highly regarded and extremely popular, appearing either in combination with other meats, or on their own as in the following recipes.

◆

TURKEY IN MOLE POBLANO

The Mexican word for turkey is not the spanish 'pava', but 'guajolote', which admirably describes the nosie these fowl make. Turkeys are, of course, natives of the Americas: the name 'turkey-fowl' was the result of misunderstandings and

sloppy research on the part of those English-speaking Europeans who first encountered them.
This is a royally complicated dish – literally, because chocolate was the food of Aztec kings and high priests. Commercial chocolate moles are very good, but this is better.

◆

S E R V E S   6 – 1 2

1 3·5 kg/8 lb turkey, cut into serving pieces
1 dozen ancho or pasilla chillies (see note)
4 tbsp sesame seeds
$\frac{1}{2}$ tsp coriander seeds
2 onions, chopped
4 cloves garlic, peeled and chopped
1 cup blanched almonds
$\frac{1}{2}$ cup raisins
$\frac{1}{2}$ tsp ground cloves
$\frac{1}{2}$ tsp ground cinnamon
3 sprigs fresh coriander
$\frac{1}{2}$ tsp anise
1 tortilla
3 medium tomatoes, peeled, de-seeded and chopped
4 tbsp lard
60 g/2 oz dark (unsweetened) chocolate
(some recipes use Mexican chocolate)
Salt and pepper

◆ Boil the turkey, in just enough salted water; simmer for one hour. Save 2 cups of the stock. Dry the turkey pieces thoroughly (paper towels are useful) and fry them, a few at a time, in the lard.

◆ Prepare the chillies as described on page 15. Ideally, you should use 6 anchos, 4 pasillas and 4 mulatos, but you will be doing well to get anchos *or* pasillas in most places.

◆ Toast the sesame seeds in a dry pan, shaking constantly. In a mortar, grind *half* of them to break their shells. Also toast and grind the coriander seeds.

◆ In a blender, purée together the ground sesame seeds and the following: onions, garlic, almonds, raisins, cloves, cinnamon, coriander (seeds and leaves), anise, tortilla, chillies and tomatoes.

◆ Cook this purée in the lard remaining in the frying pan or skillet (you may need to add another tablespoon of fat). Stir constantly, over a fairly high heat, for five minutes; then add the broth, the chocolate (broken into small pieces, or grated), and pepper and salt to taste. Cook over a low heat until the chocolate melts. The sauce should be quite thick – like American heavy cream, or somewhere between English single and double cream.

◆ Arrange the turkey in a flameproof casserole or Dutch oven; pour over the sauce; and cook at about 90°C/200°F/ Gas $\frac{1}{4}$ inside the oven, or over the lowest possible heat on top, for half to three-quarters of an hour. Garnish with the remaining toasted sesame seeds. With tortillas, beans and rice, this serves a dozen people, or six very hungry ones.

AVES CON CHILES

(Poultry with Chillies)

S E R V E S   4

4 cups/500 g/1 lb cooked chicken or turkey
4 poblano chillies
1 large red onion, chopped
2–3 tbsp lard or olive oil
1 cup/225 ml/8 fl oz sour cream
1 cup/200–250 g/6–8 oz grated (shredded)
Cheddar or Jack cheese
Salt and pepper

◆ You can use any leftover cooked poultry, diced or shredded; the super-de-luxe version of this dish, shown here, uses shredded chicken breasts.

◆ Blister and peel the chillies as described on page 15. Remove veins and seeds; dice.

◆ Cook the onion in the oil or lard until it is translucent. Add the chicken and the chillies. Cook until both are warm, stirring frequently – about 5 minutes.

◆ Add the sour cream and grated cheese. Season to taste. Stir constantly until the cheese melts – about 2 or 3 minutes.

OPPOSITE: Cooking mole in Mexico state; BELOW: Aves con Chiles.

CHICKEN CILANTRO

This is an elegantly simple dish. It is rather rich, so it is ideal as part of a long-drawn-out comida, *where each course is fairly small. A large serving might be overwhelming!*

◆

SERVES 4 – 6

**4 small, boned, skinless chicken breasts
1 small onion
At least 1 clove garlic
2 tablespoons chopped coriander leaves
4 tablespoons olive oil or butter
(or a mixture of the two)
Salt and pepper**

◆ Chop the onion and garlic, and fry them together in the olive oil and/or butter until the onion is, in the Spanish term, 'crystalline' (tender and transparent).

◆ Cut the chicken into cubes about one inch (2 to 3 cm) on a side. Fry with the onion and garlic until the chicken is cooked through: this should take no more than 5–10 minutes, depending on the temperature and the size of the cubed chicken. The meat should be browned slightly on the outside, but only in places. Add the chopped coriander leaves; stir for a few seconds to coat; serve. The pan juices are the usual sauce: for a much stronger-flavoured (and darker-coloured) sauce, deglaze the pan with half a glass of dry white wine or vermouth.

◆ Serve with plain boiled rice: enough for 4 to 6 people, depending on what else you are serving.

POLLO EN SALSA DE PIPIAN

(Chicken in Pumpkin-seed Sauce)

**3 ancho chillies
2 cloves garlic
4 cups/1 1/32 fl oz chicken stock
½ cup/125 g/4 oz peanut butter
1 cup/225 g/8 oz pumpkin seeds (pipian)
3 corn tortillas, torn into pieces
4 chicken quarters, cooked (boiled)**

◆ Prepare the chillies as described on page 15. When they are soft, drain. In a blender, combine them with all the other ingredients except the chicken. Process to a smooth paste. Do this in instalments if your blender won't handle the lot.

◆ Place chicken in a flameproof casserole or Dutch oven; pour the pipian sauce over it. Cook over a low heat for 25 minutes, or in the oven at 120°C/250°F/Gas ½ for about an hour, stirring occasionally.

LEFT: Chicken Cilantro;
OPPOSITE: Fiesta in Huejofango.

POULTRY

DESSERTS

Round off your meal with a postre or dessert if you still have any appetite left. Here is a small selection of the most popular dishes from Mexican kitchens.

◆

FLAN

'Flan' is a baked caramel-topped custard. It can be made with unreduced milk, for a lighter texture; reduced milk, which is traditional; or condensed milk, which is quicker and which is what most modern Mexican working people use.

◆

S E R V E S   6 – 1 0

9 cups/2 l/3½ pt milk
1 cup/250 g/8 oz sugar for sweetening
2 tbsp sugar for caramel, or more
6–8 large eggs
6 large egg yolks
1 tsp vanilla extract

◆ Add the first amount of sugar (1 cup) to the milk. Bring to the boil. Reduce the milk to half its original volume,

simmering and stirring regularly. This takes about 45 minutes.

◆ In a heavy non-stick saucepan, melt 2 tablespoons of sugar for the caramel. Holding the pan above the flame, shake constantly. Slowly, the sugar will form into clumps, then melt to a uniform dark honey-brown. Pour this into a metal pie-dish, and roll it around to coat the inside. (Before adding the caramel some people spray the inside of the dish with a cooking oil, or butter it lightly, to prevent sticking.) If you are making individual flans (this will make 6–10), you will need to melt two or three times as much sugar to coat the interiors of all of them. Let the caramel cool to room temperature.

◆ Beat the whole eggs, yolks and vanilla together until smooth and uniform. Slowly, beat in the hot reduced milk. Strain into mould(s), and allow to cool to room temperature.

◆ Stand the mould(s) in a baking pan containing about 5–7 cm (2–3 in) of water. this prevents burning. Cook at about 175°C/350°F/Gas 4 until the custard is just set – about half an hour for individual flans, three-quarters of an hour for a large one. Let the flan cook in the water bath.

◆ For the best chance of releasing the flan unbroken, chill it thoroughly and run a very thin knife around the edge – a very narrow palette knife is ideal. Go all the way to the bottom of the mould. Then, place the plate upside-down on top of the mould; invert, and hope for the best. You should feel a slight shock as the flan comes out and lands on the plate.

FLAN WITH CONDENSED MILK

This recipe, using sweetened condensed milk, is the usual way that Mexican working people make flan at home.

◆

SERVES 6

2 tbsp sugar (for caramel)
2 250 g/8–10 oz cans sweetened condensed milk
6 eggs
1 tsp vanilla
Grated nutmeg

◆ Prepare the caramel as for the previous recipe. Coat the mould, and cool to room temperature.
◆ Beat the milk, eggs and vanilla together thoroughly. Pour into the mould. Top with grated nutmeg.
◆ Cook as above, either in the oven or in a *bain-marie* on a hotplate or gas-burner. Cooking time is about 30 minutes. Allow to cool to room temperature; chill in the refrigerator, and turn out as before.

OPPOSITE: Flan; BELOW: Platanos Fritos con ron.

PLANTANOS

Fried or baked plantanos are a popular Mexican dessert. They need to be fried in deep, hot oil until they are thoroughly golden, or they will still be tough. Alternatively, bananas may suit most palates better. Lard is one of the best fats for frying, and leaves no unpleasant taste: use it very hot.
You may also care to try baking the plantanos or bananas. It takes a surprisingly long time for the bananas to cook and soften: a quarter of an hour at 160°C/325°F/Gas 3. Bake four bananas with the following ingredients:

◆

SERVES 4

¼ cup/60 g/2 oz granulated sugar
½ tsp cinnamon
4 tbsp/60 g/2 oz cubed butter

VARIATIONS

▶ For extra luxury, try any of the following:
▶ Top with whipped cream and cinnamon.
▶ Make a banana split with the cooked banana (split it *before* you cook it!)
▶ Flame the cooked banana in rum. If you use 151° proof rum, this may be interesting – the stuff burns like lighter-fuel!

CAKES AND COOKIES

Mexicans enjoy a wide range of pastries, which are usually something between a cake and a cookie in Norteamericano eyes. As often as not, they are bought from the local store; these three are easy enough to make at home.

◆

GALLETAS DE MEDIA LUNE

M A K E S   1 0 – 1 2

4 cups/450 g/1 lb plain (all-purpose) flour
2 scant tsp baking powder
200 g/7 oz butter
100 g/3½ oz sugar
2 eggs
1 cup/225 ml/8 fl oz milk
1¼ cups/150 g/5 oz flour (for rolling)
Strawberry jam for filling

◆ Sift the flour and baking powder together and make a ring with it on the work surface; in the centre put the butter, sugar and eggs. Mix well by hand, adding milk as necessary, to make a thick, smooth dough. Roll out thinly – 6 mm (¼ in). Cut into shapes with a biscuit or cutter: make at least two of each shape. Cook at about 175°C/350°F/Gas 4 until golden – about 10 to 20 minutes.
◆ Sandwich together in pairs with jam when cold.

POLVORONES

(Cinnamon Cakes)

M A K E S   2 0 – 2 4

100 g/3½ oz sugar
1 cup/225 g/8 oz lard
2 eggs
4 cups/450 g/1 lb plain (all-purpose) flour
1 tsp baking powder
Sugar for sprinkling
1 heaped tsp powdered cinnamon

◆ Cut the sugar into the lard. Add the eggs and beat well. Sift the flour with the baking powder; mix well. Form into balls; flatten with the fingers; sprinkle with sugar and powdered cinnamon.
◆ Bake at 175°C/350°F/Gas 4 for 25 minutes for cookies 7·5–10 cm (3–4 in) diameter, or 15 minutes for smaller ones. The big ones are more traditional.

V A R I A T I O N S

▶ Work food colouring into the dough.
▶ Add cinnamon to the dough.
▶ Use vegetable shortening.
▶ Roll in coloured sugar or 'hundreds of thousands'.

OPPOSITE, ABOVE: A
selection of pastries with the
traditional hot chocolate drink;
BELOW: Churros;
RIGHT: Polverones.

CHURROS

Churros are a sort of linear doughnut, widely sold at churrerias where they are cooked to order. Making them at home is really only worth while if you need a churro fix and cannot get them locally; they are extremely addictive.

◆

MAKES 10 – 20

1 cup/225 ml/8 fl oz water
1 tbsp sugar
Salt
1¼ cups/130 g/5 oz plain (all-purpose) flour
½ tsp baking powder
1 egg
2 tbsp butter
Lard for frying – about 5 cm/2 in deep in a big pan
Granulated sugar for rolling
½ tsp ground cinnamon (optional)

◆ Bring the water to the boil, with 1 tablespoon of sugar and a pinch of salt. Sift the flour and baking powder together: dump into the boiling water, all at once. Beat furiously with a wooden spoon until smooth – this is long, hard work. Add the egg, and 2 tablespoons of butter. Beat again: the mixture will be slightly thinner, but still dough-like and not runny. It should have a satiny, resilient consistency.

◆ Place in a *strong* forcing-bag: a weak one may burst as you squeeze out the mixture, which is again hard work. A star-shaped nozzle is traditional. Alternatively, shape them with your fingers – this is also traditional.

◆ Heat the lard very hot: almost 200°C/400°F. Squeeze out 15 cm (6 in) lengths of dough, and fry until deep golden. If you curtail the frying time, they will be doughy in the middle. Remove from the oil with tongs; drain; and roll in granulated sugar, with or without cinnamon added.

◆ In Mexican shops you can buy churro mix, which requires only that you add water. The results are very good indeed – and no need to work so hard.

NON-ALCOHOLIC DRINKS

*A small selection of drinks, both to accompany your
Mexican meal, and to enjoy separately.*

◆

REFRESCOS

*Refrescos are blended fruit drinks, mixed with cold water
and served either over ice, or well chilled. Some of the
combinations are unexpected, though.*

◆

REFRESCO ROSADO

**4 medium-size carrots
3 thick slices pineapple, peeled
1 tbsp finely chopped walnuts**

◆ Peel the carrots and dice roughly. Dice the pineapple.
Liquidize in a blender; dilute with about 4 cups/1 1/32 fl oz
water, and serve over crushed ice. Garnish with walnuts.

REFRESCO DE PEPINO Y PINA

**2–3 small peeled cucumbers
3 thick slices pineapple
Sugar to taste**

◆ Make as for Refresco Rosado, with a similar amount of
water. Use selzer water (soda water) if you like.

CHOCOLATE

*The 'food of the gods' is a Central-American delicacy. The
most readily available blend is probably Ibarra, which is
strongly sweetened and flavoured with cinnamon and
almonds. Follow the directions on the packet: two wedges
per cup for regular-strength, more (you can double the
strength) if you're an addict. Heat full-cream milk almost
to boiling; tip it into a blender; and mix thoroughly.*

◆

ATOLE

*Atole is a very Mexican drink, and is made in various ways;
but it is only fair to warn you that not everyone likes it. Its
base is masa, the same stuff from which tortillas are made:
if you cannot get fresh masa, mix about 80 g (3 oz) of masa
harina with two or three tablespoons of hot (not boiling)
water.*

◆

**100 g/4 oz masa
1 ¼ cups/300 ml/10 fl oz water
2 cups/450 ml/16 fl oz milk
60–90 g/2–3 oz piloncillo sugar, chopped**

◆ Mix the masa with-the water in a blender; empty the
blender into a saucepan. Add the milk and coarsely chopped
piloncillo. (If you can't get piloncillo, use 3 tablespoons of
dark brown sugar and half a tablespoon of molasses or
treacle.) Heat, whisking frequently, until the piloncillo is
completely dissolved.

A B O V E : Fresh fruit is a vital ingredient in drinks as well as food dishes;
O P P O S I T E : Taking time for refreshment in Inchitan.

V A R I A T I O N S

▶ For chocolate atole, add one 100 g (3½ oz) tablet of Mexican sweet chocolate, roughly chopped, along with the piloncillo.

▶ Innumerable variations are possible. You can vary the proportions of milk and water; you can increase or decrease the quantities of liquid, for a thicker or thinner atole; you can add a little crushed aniseed; you can use finely-ground nuts instead of chocolate (add cinnamon or nutmeg before serving); you can increase or decrease the sweetness; you can substitute chopped pineapple and water for the milk; you can even use strawberry purée. All are traditional. For a non-traditional variation, mix the atole with black coffee – one quarter to one half as much coffee as atole.

COFFEE

Cafe americano is black coffee; cafe con leche is brewed double-strength, then diluted with equal quantities of hot milk; and there are some interesting cafes de olla, where the coffee is boiled in an earthenware pot with various other ingredients, then filtered for serving. For a sample cafe de olla, take the following:

◆

4 cups/1 l/32 fl oz water
60 g/2 oz dark-roasted coffee
5 cm/2 in roll of cinnamon bark
120–150 g/4–5 oz piloncillo sugar, chopped

◆ In a glass or earthenware vessel, bring to a boil the water together with the cinnamon and piloncillo. (If you can't get piloncillo, use 120 g (4 oz) dark brown sugar and 1 teaspoon molasses or treacle.) Stir occasionally to help dissolve the sugar.

◆ When the water is boiling, remove from the heat. Add the coffee; stir; and let steep for five minutes. Strain into mugs. Other possible flavouring agents include aniseed; ground coriander seed; a clove, or even a wedge of chocolate.

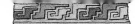

ALCOHOLIC DRINKS

Exotic cocktails are part of the mystique of Mexican culture, which also boasts a number of beers which are ideal accompaniments to the dishes in this book. The Mexican wines however are really only for true afficionados . . .

BEER

Mexican beer is deservedly very well regarded in the United States, where it is markedly superior to the domestic product. Some Mexican beers are much better than others, though: Bohemia, Dos Equis Dark and Modelo Negra are probably the strongest-flavoured. Some others really need the lime with which they are sometimes served. Squeezing a wedge of lime into an insipid beer gives a Mexican tang. Outside the United States or Mexico, Mexican beers are usually overpriced. Also, they are not particularly distinguished: many are no better than weak British lager, and most people would prefer European beers unless there is a Mexican beer they particularly like. By all means try them, but equally, do not be afraid to experiment with and serve local lagers instead.

WINES

Historically, to call Mexican wines 'undistinguished' would be unbridled flattery: you were lucky if one bottle in four was worth drinking. Some of the newer wineries are producing very much better wines, but poor storage and handling often reduces these to the standards of twenty and thirty years ago: Mexico is not really a wine-drinking nation, which is reflected in its wine.

This does not mean that wine and Mexican food should not be consumed together, though. Generally, robust Californian 'jug' wines and Eastern European wines go best with Mexican food: subtler wines are often overwhelmed. Modern Mexican wines are often very drinkable if they have not been mis-handled.

SPIRITS

Tequila is the first drink that most people associate with Mexico. In practice, tequila is mostly a working-man's drink, something to get drunk on. The traditional way to drink tequila is to put a little salt on your wrist; lick it off; take a mouthful of tequila; and follow it up with a bite on a wedge of lime or lemon. Only the uncharitable would add that this is a good way to disguise the taste.

Mezcal, charanda and sotol are very similar to tequila but are made from different varieties of maguey. The most familiar form of maguey is probably the 'century plant', with its huge sword-like leaves. Most maguey for distilling is smaller.

Mexican brandy is pretty good – again, some brands are much better than others – and this is what better-off spirits drinkers generally prefer in Mexico. Ron, or rum, is mostly surprisingly good. The strength varies widely; a full-strength ($80°$ proof/40 per cent alcohol) habanero anejo is as good a rum as you will find anywhere.

Sugar-cane also forms the basis for the $190°$ proof (95 per cent pure) alcohol that is made into rompope (see overleaf), as well as being mixed with chocolate and fresh milk or even fruit juice. Perhaps surprisingly, you can actually taste the difference between this stuff and the $190°$ proof grain spirit that is obtainable in some areas of the United States.

Mexican liqueurs (licores) exist in a wide variety of flavours and colours; they are mostly infusions made from various fruits, spices, etc, in $190°$ proof alcohol.

PULQUE AND CHICHA

Pulque is a fermented cactus 'beer', again made from the maguey. It is increasingly hard to find in Mexico, let alone elsewhere. It is a cloudy fluid with an unusual taste and a very good vitamin content – it's actually very good for you.

Chicha was traditionally made from fresh corn kernels, chewed by the women of the tribe (according to some, by the prettiest virgins), then spat into an olla. The salivary enzymes, together with natural yeasts, caused it to ferment into a thick, foamy alcoholic beverage which was traditionally served at weddings.

If you can't muster an adequate supply of virgins, try making this instead:

◆

1 large pineapple
500 g/1 lb white sugar
6 limes, sliced
½ tsp each cinnamon, cloves and nutmeg
1 gallon (US)/⅚ gallon (UK)/4 litres water

◆ Remove the spiky top from the pineapple. Wash, chop and mash the rest, including the skin. Dissolve the sugar in the water; add the remaining ingredients. Leave to ferment in a clay, glass or plastic vessel: rely on natural yeasts, or add a packet of wine yeast from a winemaking shop. It will resemble pineapple-flavoured cider, and will be ready to drink in anything between a day and a week, depending on the temperature of the room (or refrigerator) and the stage at which you like to drink it.

OPPOSITE: A selection of Mexican beers; ABOVE: Pineapple Beer.

RIGHT: Margarita; OPPOSITE: Tequila Sunrise.

COCKTAILS

Cocktails seem to be a part of the image of Mexico; relaxed, enjoyable, and perhaps slightly risqué. *If you are serving a Mexican meal to friends, a few cocktails may help to get them in the mood – but remember, these things are often stronger than they taste, and they go down remarkably easily.*

MARGARITA

The most famous Mexican cocktail is the Margarita, which is essentially a formalization of the salt-lime-tequila ritual mentioned on page 91. The proportions can vary widely, but this is a good starting point:

◆

Salt
1 measure tequila
½ measure Triple Sec
1 measure fresh lime juice

◆ Put 6 mm (¼ in) of salt in a saucer. Special Margarita salt is slightly coarser, but tastes just the same and is ridiculously expensive. Moisten the rim of a glass with a wedge of lime; twirl the rim in the salt to coat it.
◆ Shake the tequila, Triple Sec and lime juice together with cracked ice. Pour into the glass.

CUBA LIBRE

A fancy name for a rum-and-cola with a dash of lime-juice. You may however be surprised at how much difference you can make by varying the rum: in particular, try 'black' or dark rum, and Bacardi's 151° proof rum (75 per cent alcohol).

◆

30–60 ml/1–2 oz rum
180–350 ml/6–12 oz Coca-Cola or other cola drink
Juice of half a lime
2 ice cubes
Slice of lime to garnish

92

TEQUILA SUNRISE

The other Mexican cocktail that is widely known outside Mexico is the 'Tequila Sunrise'. It gets its name from the way the grenadine syrup sinks to the bottom, giving a beautiful gradation of colour.

◆

**1½ measuires tequila
6 measures orange juice
½ measure grenadine syrup**

◆ Mix the tequila and orange juice, with ice if required. Strain into a glass (ice will spoil the 'sunrise' effect). Add the grenadine, carefully. If you particularly want the sunrise to look really good, hold a small funnel so that the end is 2–3 cm (about 1 in) under the surface of the drink, then add the grenadine through that: there is less surface mixing this way.

PINA COLADA

Look in the juice section of the supermarket for coconut-pineapple juice; this will make a very much better pina colada than a 'pina colada mix', and is considerably cheaper too. Alternatively, melt a little cream of coconut in water or coconut milk (60–80 g/2–3 oz of cream of coconut to 350 ml/12 fl oz liquid), using the microwave. Whisk well. Cool. Add to an equal volume of pineapple juice.

◆

**4 cups/1 l/32 fl oz coconut-pineapple juice
100 ml/4 fl oz dark or black rum
100 ml/4 fl oz light or filtered rum**

◆ Shake well with cracked ice. Serves 6, or 12 if they have to drive home later. Some people add ⅔ cup/120 ml/4 fl oz of single (heavy) cream. Pina colada is also delicious frozen, as a dessert.

ROMPOPE

◆

**4 cups/1 l/32 fl oz milk
500 g–1 kg/1–2 lb sugar
10 egg yolks
3 cups/750 ml/24 fl oz 190° proof cane alcohol
Pinches of powdered cinnamon and grated nutmeg
1 clove**

◆ Boil together the milk, sugar and spices until reduced by at least 25 per cent of the original volume. When cool, skim, and add the alcohol, beating constantly. If you cannot get the alcohol, use a bottle of 151° proof rum or a bottle and a half of 100° proof. Beat the egg yolks until thick, then beat into the rompope. Sprinkle cinnamon or fresh-grated nutmeg (or both) on top before serving.

◆ Much as it may scandalize Americans, children are given small bowls of rompope in Mexico – and they love it. Some Mexican men add a slug of brandy to their rompope: a serious sort of drink.

GLOSSARY

ADOBADO/ADOBADA *Spiced with ADOBO sauce*

ADOBO *Pungent, spicy, vinegar-based sauce*

ALBONDIGAS *Meatballs*

ALMUERZO *Light breakfast*

ANAHEIM *Large, mild fresh chilli*

ANCHO *Type of large, leathery dried chilli*

ARBOL *Very hot dried chilli*

ARROZ *Rice*

ASADA/ASADO *Roast, grilled or seared*

ATOLE *Sweet drink thickened with MASA*

AVES *Poultry*

BIRRIA *Tender, barbecued or pot-roasted meat*

BORRACHO/BORRACHA *'Drunk'; in cooking, cooked with wine, beer or spirits*

BUDIN *Similar to lasagna, made with tortillas*

BURRITO *Large flour TORTILLA wrapped around a filling*

CALDO *Soup or thin stew*

CALIFORNIA *Large, mild chilli; usually dried*

CARNE *Meat: de res (or de vaca) is beef; de puerco is pork*

CAZUELA *Shallow earthenware cooking-pot*

CENA *Supper, evening meal*

CERVEZA *Beer*

CEVICHE *Fish pickled in lime juice*

CHAYOTE *Pear-shaped gourd or squash*

CHILE RELLENO *Stuffed fresh chilli*

CHIPOTLE *Small, hot, smoked chilli*

CHORIZO *Spicy sausage*

CHURROS *Fried cakes – a sort of linear doughnut*

CILANTRO *Coriander or 'Chinese parsley'*

COLORADO *Red; usually a tomato sauce*

COMAL *Earthenware or cast metal griddle for cooking tortillas*

COMIDA *Main meal of the day, taken in early afternoon*

ELOTE *Sweet corn, maize (fresh)*

ENTREMES *Appetizers*

ESCABECHE *Pungent pickling sauce made with vinegar*

FAJITAS *Skirt steak, marinaded and grilled*

FIDEOS *Vermicelli*

FRIJOLES *Beans. Frijoles refritos are refried beans*

GUACAMOLE *Mashed avocados*

GUAJILLO *Large dried chilli. Strong-flavoured*

HOMINY *Maize (Indian corn) treated with lye*

HUACHINANGO *Red snapper. Also guachinango. A popular fish*

HUEVOS *Eggs. Huevos Rancheros are 'ranch-style', Huevos Revueltos are scrambled*

JALAPENO *Large, very hot chilli pepper*

JICAMA *Root vegetable, something like a cross between a potato and an apple in flavour*

JICAMATE *Tomato*

LENGUA *Tongue*

MACHACA *Shredded dried beef*

MACHOMO *Similar to MACHACA, but easier to make*

MAGUEY *Sword-leaved cactus; Century Plant is a member of this family*

MANCHA MANTEL *Literally 'tablecloth-stainer'. Stew with fruit and chillies*

MASA *Maize dough*

MASA HARINA *Flour for making maize dough*

MERIENDA *Substantial 'second breakfast'*

MOLE *Sauce. Pronounced 'mow-lay'*

NEW MEXICO *Large dried chilli, slightly picante*

NOPALITOS *Cactus sprouts*

OLLA *Deep earthenware cooking-pot*

PAELLA *Seafood (and possibly other meat, etc) cooked with rice*

PASILLA *Large, mild dried chilli. Sometimes powdered*

PESCADO *Fish, after it has been caught*

PICADILLO *Beef hash – but that doesn't do it justice*

PICANTE *Spicy-hot. Muy picante is very hot; poco picante is mild*

PICO DE GALLO *Salad made of JICAMA and oranges*

PILONCILLO *Unrefined sugar*

PIPIAN *Raw, unsalted pumpkin seeds*

PLANTANO *Type of banana used in cooking*

POBLANO *Large, mild fresh chilli*

POLPO *Squid*

POSTRE *Dessert*

POZOLE *Pork with Hominy*

QUESADILLA *Cheese melted in a folded TORTILLA. A quesadilla sincronizada is two tortillas stuck together with melted cheese*

QUESO FUNDIDO *Melted cheese: cf 'fondue'*

RECADO DE BISTECK *Pungent, vinegar-based sauce*

REFRESCO *Water flavoured with fresh fruit purée*

REFRITOS *Refried beans*

REPOLLO *Cabbage*

SALSA *Sauce. Salsa cruda is uncooked sauce*

SERRANO *Very hot chilli pepper*

SOPA *Soup*

TACO *Folded TORTILLA with filling*

TAMALES *Meat wrapped in MASA and steamed in corn husks*

TOMATILLO *Looks like a green tomato, with a papery husk*

TORTILLA *Flat 'bread' made of corn or flour. A tortilla de huevo is an omelette*

TOSTADA *Fried TORTILLA with topping*

TOSTADITA *Small TOSTADA: corn-chips*

VERDE *Green; usually made with TOMATILLOS*

INDEX

MEXICAN COOKING

with Hominy 70
with zucchini 73
Pot stew 70
Poultry 59
with Chillies 81
Pozole 70
Puerco Adobado 26
Puerco con Repollo y
Elote 73
Pulque and Chica 91

Q

Quesadillas* 29
Queso Fundido* 28

R

Ranch-style Eggs 32
Ranch-style Sauce 32
Ranch-style Steak 59
Ready-made food 10–11
Recado de Bisteck 26

Refrescos 88/89
Refried beans 18
Rice 20/21
soup 49
Rompope 93
Ropa Vieja 64
Rum 91

S

Saffron 20
Salads 40/41
Salsa* 22/23
Salsa Cruda* 22/23
Salsa de Jicamate 25
Salsa Ranchera 32
Salsa Verde 22
Seviche see CEVICHE
Scrambled eggs 35
Shredded beef stew 65
Siesta 14
Sopa de Albondigas see

CALDO DE ALBONDIGAS
Sopa de Ajo 44
Sopa de Arroz 49
Sopa de Fideos 47
Sopas* see SOUPS
Secas see DRY SOUPS
Soups 14, 44–47
Spanish rice 20
Spice-grinder 14/15
Spices 10–13
Spirits 91
Steak Tartare 60
Stuffed Bell Peppers 37

T

'Tablecloth-stainer' 74
Tamales 78/79
Tamale pie 79
'Tex-Mex' Chilli con
carne 63
Tequila 91

Sunrise 93
Tomatillos 11, 66
Tomato sauce 25
Tongue 60
Tortilla 16–17
Budin de 50
de Huevo 32
frying 16
press 17
soup 49
Tostadas* 16/17, 30
Turkey in Mole Poblano 81

V

Vegetables 42/43
Vermicelli soup 47

W

White bean soup 19
Wines 91

CREDITS:

Food Photography: Steve Alley and Amber Wisdom;
Roger Hicks and Frances Schultz; John Norton
Food Preparation: Roger Hicks, Frances Schultz, Marion
Schultz, Juana Ibarra
Landscape Photographs supplied by Liba Taylor

ACKNOWLEDGEMENTS:

We would like to thank the people of the parish of Our
Lady of Guadalupe, Guadalupe, California, and especially
the following (in alphabetical order):
Maria-Luisa Amarillas, *for recipes*
Juan Brad, *for many recipes and ideas*
Margarita Fausta, *for recipes*
Juana Ibarra, *for recipes, tamales and assistance*
Olivia Jaime, *for recipes and ideas*
Rosalia Perez-Gomez, *for initial setting-up*
Manuel Ramos, *for recipes, explanations and co-ordination*
Nellie Ramos, *for recipes and assistance*
Padre Julio Roman of Our Lady of Guadalupe
Marion Schultz, *for recipes and assistance*

96